Reviews by Cat Ellington

Books by Cat Ellington

REVIEWS BY CAT ELLINGTON: THE COMPLETE ANTHOLOGY, VOL. 1

REVIEWS BY CAT ELLINGTON: THE COMPLETE ANTHOLOGY, VOL. 2

THE MAKING OF DUAL MANIA: FILMMAKING CHICAGO STYLE

REVIEWS BY CAT ELLINGTON – THE COMPLETE ANTHOLOGY LIMITED EDITION HOLIDAY GIFT SET (BOOKS 1 & 2)

REVIEWS BY CAT ELLINGTON: THE COMPLETE ANTHOLOGY, VOL. 3

Reviews by Cat Ellington
The Complete Anthology, Vol. 3

Cat Ellington

Quill Pen Ink Publishing
THE BEAUTY OF EXPRESSION™
CHICAGO

Copyright ©2019 Cat Ellington

PAPERBACK ISBN: 978-1-7334421-0-7
HARDCOVER ISBN: 978-1-7370971-7-4

Library of Congress Control Number: 2022362727

All rights reserved. No part of this publication may be reproduced or transmitted in any form or by any means electronic, including photocopy, recording, or any information storage and retrieval system, without permission in writing from the copyright owner.

Cover design: Hues of the Reviews
Vol. 3 Hue: Bubblegum Yum
The Cat Ellington Literary Collection

Published by Quill Pen Ink Publishing
Chicago, Illinois, USA
https://quill-pen-ink-publishing.business.site/

Quill Pen Ink Publishing, 2019

Hardcover Edition: October 2021

Printed in the U.S.A.

Dedication

To Judy Mui—
Golden Gate princess, special friend,
and the grooviest China girl in all the world

Foreword

Those of us who have not only a love of reading but also a deep affection (and respect) for the written word know far too well that the craft can at times be both exhilarating and challenging. It all depends upon what day a writer happens to run into some mental roadblocks. But then there are also times when one happens upon a writer whose clarity of insight, along with their indescribable gift of observation into human nature, causes us to see things and people differently.

Case in point: Cat Ellington. It is through such a lens that Cat Ellington is perceived. I have known her for quite some time and am thoroughly familiar with her work as a versatile songwriter/composer, poet, author, and film casting director. But when Cat began to convey to me - many years ago - that she had been creating book reviews since the (tender) age of eleven, I was speechless - because I hadn't expected that literary criticism was among her many extraordinary talents in the arts.

While I am immensely impressed by her (adroit) insight and her bawdy sense of humor, what I genuinely admire about the Cat Ellington review is the nurturing and empathetic outlook that it presents. It says a lot about its author and her exceptional ability to understand - through great spiritual wisdom - the deepest (and sometimes darkest) innermost workings of Mankind - by way of the human body, and the human mind, and the human soul. This quality is what sets Cat Ellington apart from all the rest. What also makes the Cat Ellington review so unique is the way she incorporates a vast spectrum of references for each critique, including Biblical scriptures, movies, television shows, and music. This method is her way of highlighting key points in both plot and character.

That said, I will encourage all of you readers to buckle up and have fun because you're in for the word-slingin' ride of your life - as only Cat Ellington can navigate it.

Joseph Strickland

Writer/Director

Preface

Hello again, my dearest readers. It has been exactly one year since the release of *Reviews by Cat Ellington: The Complete Anthology, Vol. 1*. And in the time since, we've proudly published two more books in the progressive series, including *Reviews by Cat Ellington: The Complete Anthology, Vol. 2* and *Reviews by Cat Ellington – The Complete Anthology Limited Edition Holiday Gift Set (Books 1 & 2)*, respectively.
And I must say that the experience has been nothing short of fabulous.

I thank all of you who have gone way beyond the call to support this series. Whether by way of a kind word spoken or otherwise. Thank you so much.

As I continue onward in my journey with this succession, I am honored to present *Reviews by Cat Ellington: The Complete Anthology, Vol. 3* for your reading pleasure.
Yet another great blessing bestowed upon me, book three represents my arrival into the digital age: Internet platforms, social media platforms, mobile applications, and, of course, eBooks. While the analyses in books 1 & 2 were written in an old-fashioned way—longhand—the thirty examinations that comprise this collection, though researched and noted manually, were all structured (digitally) on laptops and smart devices. It was a whole new animal, yes, but it was fun. And I quickly got the hang of it, even though there were many frustrating trials.

In my introduction, I will share some of the irritating roadblocks that I encountered along the route of my transfer to the Internet—where it pertains to my written analyses—and what I learned from many irreparable mistakes.

My dearest men and women, take a load off and enjoy yourselves. And I hope that all of you will enjoy reading this work as much as I did writing it.

Lovingly,

Cat Ellington

Acknowledgments

First and foremost—and always first and foremost—I humbly ascribe glory to my Lord and my God for all of His great gifts and blessings. For without Him, I could do nothing. And of this fact, I will forever be well aware. Praise be to the Father, the Son, and the Holy Spirit—the one and ONLY Divine Trinity.

Joe, thank you, baby. Thank you for providing your shoulder to me when I needed it to lean on. And thank you for all the wise words that you so generously shared with me over the many years that I've known you. I also thank you for your brilliant sense of humor: for you know how to make a gal bust-up in laughter. You are one of the best people. And I am so blessed to have you in my life. I love you as both my hubby and dearest friend.

Nathaniel, Nairobi, and Naras, I love you. Mama is so proud of all of you. And I am so honored to say that you three are the fruit of my womb, my groovy litter, my kiddens. And I love you always.

Freddie and Maurice, thank you, my beloved brothers, for all of your support, love, and encouragement. I am truly blessed to have both of you in my life. For ours is a beautiful fellowship.

John and the entire team at Google, thank you! You guys are the best—especially you, John. Thank you.

Thank you, team AUTHORSdb! Thank you so much.

As always, thank you to my readers.
Y'all stay groovy now, ya hear?

Love forever,

Cat Ellington

Introduction

Dear reader,

As *Reviews by Cat Ellington: The Complete Anthology, Vol. 3* marks the beginning of my foray into a brand new world of digitalization in literature, I thought that I would take the opportunity to shed a bit of light on my earlier experience with this new technology.

Before 2012, my entire library consisted of only print books in both hardcover and paperback formats. And I loved it. For over thirty years, I had only read physical books, and I loved it. I loved holding my books in hand and running my fingers over the glossy covers. I loved the habit of licking the tip of my index finger to turn every new page. I loved the "crisp" smell of the books (if the books were newly-purchased). I loved all of my stylish bookmarks, too. I loved the *feel* of the book's weight in my hand. And so on. I loved everything about the reading experience in the days of old. But once the so-called eReader—designed to carry massive digital libraries of so-called eBooks—came into being, that all changed.

While I admired this new form of technology, you know, the concept of reading electronic books on electronic devices, I'll admit that I had to get used to it. During the first couple of weeks, I kept tapping my tongue with the tip of my index finger to turn the pages, forgetting that the books were in a digital format and not printed. But that all soon subsided. Readers were also able to leave ratings and reviews at the end of each book, which I liked because the method allowed me to compose my (comprehensive) analyses by typing them onto my selected device rather than structuring them in longhand. The afforded convenience was addictive. And the entire process had been one smooth sail.

Indeed, everything had been going just fine until I decided to perform a factory reset on my old device. It was the same device on which I'd kept all of my reviews. They were in a folder in a reading app. But after the reset, they were gone - forever.

A factory reset restores a device to its original factory settings. And that was what I had wanted to do at the time. But what I failed to understand then is that I would have had to back up my files to protect them during the factory reset. And I did not do that. So in the wake of the restoration, I lost my reviews. And I cried for days about losing them. It hurt me that they were gone.

My book reviews I liken to my song works. And losing any of my examinations is the same to me as losing one of my song works.

The emotional pain that the loss of my reviews caused me was nothing short of anguishing. And trust, my dear reader, that I have never forgotten my error. For if truth be told, it was one of the biggest mistakes from which I have ever had to learn.

Structuring *Reviews by Cat Ellington: The Complete Anthology, Vol. 3* has been perhaps my most challenging effort yet because I had to start from scratch on any number of my critiques.

I had to rewrite some of the reviews (in this collection) from the pages of my handwritten notes. And for this reason, the original release date—April 2019—was pushed back until now.

While I am grateful to be done with this phase of my contribution, it is my profound hope that you will enjoy this collection and appreciate all of the hard work that it took to bring it to fruition.

Once again, I thank you for your interest in this, my respective contribution to the field of literature.

All my love,

Cat Ellington

Sketch of Cat Ellington by Joseph Strickland

January 1, 2013

Table of Contents

Dedication

Foreword

Preface

Acknowledgments

Introduction

Chapter 1: Evolution in the New Era

Chapter 2: Learning the Fundamentals of Digitalization

Chapter 3: Getting the Hang of It

Chapter 4: Slowly But Surely

Chapter 5: In Flourishing Mode

Chapter 6: Now Thriving

Coming September 2019: More Imaginative Than Ordinary Speech: The Poetry of Cat Ellington

About the Author

Chapter 1
Evolution in the New Era

Cat Ellington's review of Enemies and Playmates by Darcia Helle

My rating: 5 out of 5 stars

Date read: October, 2012

MEET ME AT THE BAR.

Everything is not as it seems.
Not even on the outstanding pages of this delectably romantic, albeit shamefully wicked, suspense thriller.

As the velvet curtain of its cover opens to introduce the reader to a talented ensemble—playing their parts in perfect unison with an expertly-crafted script—we make the acquaintance of our leading lady, Lauren Covington (a major in journalism at Harvard). Lauren is spending a night out on the town with her two best friends, the beautiful and ridiculously flirtatious Gina and Carrie, the techno-geek. It's a fun night out clubbing. And the three women, well, Gina and Carrie at least, are enjoying the atmosphere and all that it has to offer, including an ear-thumping sound system to which there is plenty of room to move on the massive dance floor. Not the socializing type outside of her circle, the shy Lauren, who has chosen to remain glued to the seat of her barstool, is sitting alone and watching her girls own the night. That is until Dean, the man seated on the barstool next to hers, leans over to drop a lame, drunken line – right before asking her out on a date. Of course, her answer is no - a very polite no.

Same old story. It's just another lonely evening out club-hopping with the besties. Lauren is practically bored to tears until she sees him across the room—ever so tall, confident, sexy, and solidly built—wearing a black leather jacket and loose-fitting jeans. Of all the women in the club, his piercing gaze is reserved only for Lauren Covington. And it's enough to make her blush.

Enter Jesse Ryder, a private investigator who just so happens to be in the employ of Lauren's godless father, Alex, a man she just so happens to hate with a passion. Jesse and Lauren have an inevitable mutual attraction. And they soon meet and greet over drinks at the bar. In time, Gina and Carrie join in the conversation, making pleasantries merry. And the evening is at peace with the crowd of four. But, determined not to be outdone, fate intervenes, urging the handsome Jesse to escort the timid Lauren to the dance floor, marking the beginning of a most fervently erotic love affair - and a most-vindictive rage.

LOOKS CAN BE DECEIVING.

The Covington family appear to have it all to those who peer into their affluent lives from the outside: unlimited money, a palatial home, only the finest of luxuries, a close-knit bond of unconditional love, and enviable respectability.

But it is all a lie.
It is all one hellish façade of a lie.

Physically, Alex Covington is a handsome, expensively-attired, upstanding, and phenomenally successful attorney at law. But spiritually, Alex Covington—this tale's hideously loathsome antagonist—is an individual prone to reprehensible evil.
A human host in the extremes of passive/aggressive dysfunction, Alex Covington nurtures only a few nauseating aspirations, one of which includes making everyday life a Hadean experience for his immediate family at home. Not one who fancies being challenged or contradicted, Alex Covington elects to enforce (and then reinforce) his alpha-male authority by way of both harsh words and violent action. And now aware of the romantic involvement between his only daughter and his archenemy *(that bastard, Jesse Ryder),* Alex Covington, clad in Armani, becomes the ultimate bringer of misery and destruction on all of those who dare to drift into his arrogant and unchaste orbit, including the young men intent on rebelling against his scandalous wishes: his son, Stephen Covington, and his intolerable employee, Jesse Ryder.

THE SUPPORT TEAM.

Rounding out a splendid, top-billed ensemble—who will remain imprinted on the reader's psyche long after the final page unfurls—are the following:

- Kara Covington, who stuns as a desperate wife and a mother beaten into submission

- Suzanne Sampson, a blonde bombshell and faithful secretary to Alex Covington

- Chris Nyles, a convicted murderer and former associate of Alex Covington

- Tim O'Leary, best friend to Jesse Ryder and fellow hard-nosed detective hot on the heels of depraved criminality

These are all offset by only a small troupe of supporting and bit players, including:

- Kevin Fuller, the good-looking, badass friend of Stephen Covington and candyman to the rich and bored

- Paul Stosh, Lauren's empathetic boss

- Captain James Barnes, a mutual acquaintance of Alex Covington and officer on the take

- Marc Wilkes, a true guardian angel if there were ever one

FLATTERING WORDS.

Striking one conniving blow after another, the Boston-based *Enemies and Playmates* is a fictional time bomb recommended for every fan of romantic thrillers.

Darcia Helle gives it her very best with this novel. And I am beyond honored to have received a complimentary copy. What an exceptional effort, Darcia Helle!

Five tyrannical stars.

Cat Ellington's review of Heller (Heller, #1) by J.D. Nixon

My rating: 5 out of 5 stars

Date read: October, 2012

A QUIET GEM.

I first read *Heller* (*Heller, #1*) via the *Kindle* app on my smartphone in October of 2012 - which was nearly a year after the novel's release. And although I'd composed a more detailed review of the work in the wake of completing it, I still cannot find my original review. Therefore, I have concluded that I had perhaps stored it away with a small batch of other reviews missing from my collection in my second city of residence. That or the examination is lost forever.
Regardless of whatever the case may be, I am inclined to render this exciting action thriller the genuine praise - of which it is well-deserving.

In brief, *Heller* (*Heller, #1*) is a memorable tale starring Matilda "Tilly" Chalmers. Tilly plays a young security specialist who is way up the industry ladder to obtain a successful career in her field of expertise at Heller's Security & Surveillance. But as Tilly gets comfortable in her new job, chaos arrives to test her to the furthest limit.

Heller (*Heller, #1*) is a beautiful dialogue seeped in romantic undertones between Tilly and her powerful and no-nonsense boss, Mr. Heller, vengeance, deception, lies, and cold-blooded murder.

A charming and cozy narrative that I am sure many action thriller fans will enjoy immensely, *Heller* (*Heller, #1*) is a quietly precious gem worthy of not only a lazy afternoon read but also my loftiest ranking.
Great work, J.D. Nixon.

Five armed-and-totally-dangerous stars.

Cat Ellington's review of Deadly Offerings (Deadly Trilogy, #1) by Alexa Grace

My rating: 4 out of 5 stars

Date read: October, 2012

STALKED BY A KILLER.

Much like J.D. Nixon's *Heller* (*Heller, #1*), *Deadly Offerings* (*Deadly Trilogy, #1*) had been yet another effort in my brand new library of eBooks that I'd completed during the earlier days of my delve into the Internet sphere. It was October of 2012, to be exact, that I'd received this fictional work free of charge via *Barnes & Noble*. And immediately taken by the title's description, I dove—headfirst—into the plot, soon falling madly in love with its gorgeous leading lady, Anne Mason, as well as with its fast-paced suspense and its intriguing mystery.

Deadly Offerings (*Deadly Trilogy, #1*) is a good book that I enjoyed reading back in 2012. Unfortunately, though, I lost the original review in the factory reset I spoke about earlier. On these gripping pages, the plot orbits around a psychotic murderer who hunts and kills his victims before discarding their remains in a cornfield. The cornfield is on a farm owned by Anne. And the killer aims to send her a morbid message that she will soon be among the dead.

While it is unfortunate that I cannot locate the small collection of analyses; nevertheless, I had to honor this fascinating psychological thriller with a critique of which it is tremendously worthy - even if it is brief.

OH, AND ANOTHER THING:

Although our leading man, Michael Brandt, annoyed me beyond what is tolerable—due to the extremities of his possessive nature towards the auburn-haired Anne—*Deadly Offerings* (*Deadly Trilogy, #1*) kept my reader enticed and thoroughly entertained from beginning to end. Aside from Michael Brandt's nettlesome actions, the narrative is splendid in ensemble and structure. And I will always be willing to add a little more wind to its stunning sails.

As an afterthought, I should perhaps add that there is no such thing as anyone being loved too much by someone else. Especially not if that person just so happens to be his or her significant other - as is the case with Michael Brandt and Anne Mason, respectively. But his performance on these pages is just a breath away from an obsessive-compulsive disorder where it concerns Anne. And for no reason other than his irritating behavior, this work has been robbed of a five-star rating.

Happy reading, all.

Cat Ellington's review of Big Girls Don't Cry by Gretchen Lane

My rating: 5 out of 5 stars

Date read: October, 2012

A WHOLE LOTTA LOVELINESS.

A few pounds overweight or not, aspiring model Gretchen Lane can be one atrociously sexy woman if only she puts her mind to it. But in the constant crosshairs of bitter scorn, malicious mockeries, and spiteful ridicule from others—strangers at that—bonding with self-esteem can be downright impossible.

Gretchen Lane is an obese twenty-four-year-old virgin who spends her days working an average job, chatting on the phone with her best friend, Michelle, and, quite naturally, eating. And until now, she has become conditioned in the flesh of her bulky weight, hiding out in her home and relieving her sexual tensions by way of erotic fantasies and a bedside pleasure chest.

Gretchen Lane is not unlike the typical fat girl, meaning a standard target of cruel and hateful mistreatment. It's the story of her life. And, unfortunately, Gretchen has grown more accustomed to it. That isn't to say she enjoys it, only that she has come to expect it. However, it isn't until after she gets assaulted by someone who throws a 32-ounce soft drink at her that she begins to realize that there has to be more to her life than this, what being called horrible names and having someone smack her in the face with a large cup filled with frigid ice and pop. There has to be more to life than that. Gretchen Lane knows this. And soon enough, she decides to do something about it. She'll hire herself a personal trainer. And together, they'll tackle her antagonistic weight down to size.

A personal trainer. She, Gretchen Lane, of all chubby gals, will have her very own personal trainer. Oh, it's going to be so exciting!

And how.

If only she knew that her future personal trainer would be the provocative, rough, and rugged Billy Mack. The buffed extraordinaire.

DON'T MESS WITH BILL.

Chubby or not, Gretchen Lane is beautiful in the eyes of her beholder, Billy Mack. And as their new friendship blossoms and grows into something more dramatically adult-themed, Billy, the man of Gretchen's erotic dreams, takes the passionate initiative, unwrapping her to reveal that special gift of man-eating love.

And boy, does he love her.

SPITFIRE AND DESIRE.

I must say that I, too, fell madly in love with Gretchen Lane throughout this short-lived tale of heat-inducing erotica—as she is perfection.

Gretchen and Billy's newfound romance is deep, wild, sweaty, and heart-pounding. And as they romp about in the intense fire of their burning desire, Gretchen will soon learn that Billy Mack's loins are not his only fierce attribute: for a rival to his (blessed) manhood is his explosive temper. Indeed, it must be that offenses come, but woe to that man by whom the offense comes, especially when Billy Mack's new girlfriend, the tubby Gretchen Lane, is the target thereof.

A REVIEWER SMITTEN.

For a work of erotic fiction with pagination of only 57, *Big Girls Don't Cry* packs a powerful punch from start to finish. And I can't imagine any pundit of the erotica genre not admiring its script and the applause-worthy performances of its memorable cast as much as I did.

Big Girls Don't Cry, a great read, indeed, was my introduction to the alluring literature of its fascinating authorship, Gretchen Lane. And it is with genuine anticipation that I look forward to making the acquaintance *Big Girls Don't Cry 2: The Emancipation of Gretchen*, its successor in the series.
My fellow reader, I highly recommend this effort for your reading pleasure. But please note that the storyline contains erotica, including anal penetration, and therefore must be approached with caution—should you be of those given to discomfort by such explicitly graphic content.

Five erect-and-lubricated stars.

Cat Ellington's review of Taken: Menage Romance by Selena Kitt

My rating: 5 out of 5 stars

Date read: October, 2012

IT'S JUST US GIRLS.

Counting all of the books that managed to remain forever embossed on my bibliophilic psyche, even long after I completed them, *Taken: Menage Romance* by Selena Kitt is among that uniquely fascinating lot.

Our leading lady, Lizzie—a youngster preparing to enroll in college—works for a telemarketing/market research firm that lays the foundation for this tightly puckered and deeply penetrating novella of erotica.
Lizzie and her older boss, Sarah (the so-called "Ice Princess"), have formed a bond both on and off the job. They share details about their private lives, they joke and laugh, and they have a good time. They are just trying to survive each passing day. Their daily schedule? It's always the same: work to home, home to work, with a little fun time in-between. And in their small office of seven employees, including Lizzie and Sarah, peace dwells safely with respect.

While Sarah, a divorcée, has been shaded and jaded by love one too many times, Lizzie herself is smack dab in the middle of a lonely relationship, if one could even call it that, with her neglectful boyfriend, Tim. This duo of attractive women, despite their age difference, are truly kindred spirits and the very best of friends. At least so far.

LET HIM IN.

David is a thirty-five-year-old divorcé and telemarketing specialist who has a thing for Sarah. After swearing off relationships in the wake of his divorce, David is now ready to give Cupid another chance. But only on one condition: bring him the whole body of Sarah on a silver platter. Both David's heart and his endowed loins ache for Sarah. But Sarah has been hurt too many times by the men in her life. The thirty-something stunner has grown cold and distant from the male species in general - preferring instead to direct her lustful affections towards other women. And on these pages, her much older vulva burns for that of the much younger Lizzie.

But is this telemarketing supervisor—the seductive Sarah—that conflicted? Does she hate men that much, or is she just fooling herself into thinking that she does? Does David secretly turn her on? Or does he genuinely disgust her? What woman in the world wouldn't cherish the feeling of being loved—wide open—by a real man? Seriously, what woman wouldn't? David wants Sarah so bad that he literally can taste her. But Lizzie is always present.

Lizzie is always right there - trapped in the middle.

Dear reader? What is every man's fantasy? David - equipped with an amazingly outstanding organ - is about to make every man's fantasy his sweaty, entangled reality.

I GET SO EMOTIONAL.

As we glide through rainy days of intense sexual escapades between the stars of this beautiful, albeit emotional, tale of erotica, we are made susceptible to the many trials that nip at Lizzie along the course of her young life. And even more so to those shattering woes that attach themselves to David and Sarah, individually.

My heart gave way after having been so incessantly tugged at by this trio of unforgettable characters. And I will love them forever.

No amount of praise for the production of this marvelous narrative will ever be sufficient for its incredibly gifted authorship, Selena Kitt.

Hands down, *Taken: Menage Romance* is one of the greatest novellas that I've ever enjoyed the pleasure of reading. Ever.

And while it is true that I love(d) this read madly—it was sexy, fun, erotic, fast-paced, and exceedingly challenging to part ways with—the dialogue's ending succeeded in throwing me for a gut-wrenching loop.

In all honesty, it took me four days to get over the brief spell of depression caused by this effort in the wake of my completing it. Four days.

With *Taken: Menage Romance*, Selena Kitt got me right here. She does a fabulous job in terms of both script and cast. And I will never forget either.

Taken: Menage Romance—destined to be listed as one of my all-time favorite works of erotic fiction—is an exceptional work that is meritable of its perfect rating here.

Five three-way stars.

Chapter 2
Learning the Fundamentals of Digitalization

Cat Ellington's review of Sharko by Ben Borland

My rating: 3 out of 5 stars

Date read: December, 2012

LONE SHARKS.

Ben Borland's *Sharko* had been yet another novel in a set of eBooks that I'd read during the earlier days of my newfound experience with the so-called eReader. It was late December of 2012 when I viewed this chilling thriller about a psychotic murderer—dubbed Sharko—who spends his free time preying on local prostitutes. Following violent acts of sexual intercourse, he kills them before feeding their remains to the sharks that prowl the waters off Coogee Heads in a twisted endeavor to conceal his diabolical crimes.

Although I'd composed a detailed (digital) review of *Sharko* in the wake of my concluding it, I seriously regret to inform you, dear reader, that the analysis was lost to me forever in a factory reset on my device. So for the objective of rendering this moderately paced—and at times intriguing—crime fiction the recognition it so rightfully deserves, I will proceed with the following:

A BIT SLOW, BUT SATISFACTORY.

Set in Sydney, Australia (during the Great Depression), *Sharko* simultaneously blends hard-boiled noir, syndicate ties, a bit of psychological suspense, and romance into one hefty script of crime fiction - complemented by a passably talented ensemble.

Here, we make the acquaintance of a somewhat memorable leading man in Detective Inspector William Gunn. And while the plot is reasonably satisfactory, it fails to validate such considerable pagination. If truth be told, *Sharko* could have also done without such a large cast as too many irrelevant players only serve to spoil any written dialogue with genuine potential.

While entertaining at times, *Sharko*, overall, is not powerful enough to command a perfect five-star rating.

Happy reading, everyone.

Cat Ellington's Review of Plain Jane: Brunettes Beware (Harbinger Mystery, #1) by Cristyn West

My rating: 2 out of 5 stars

Date read: December, 2012

NOTHING STRIKING.

My fellow reader,

When you view the tagline, '*Not for the faint of heart*,' attributed to *Plain Jane: Brunettes Beware* (*Harbinger Mystery, #1*), see that you acquire it with a grain of salt - although it could be considered the perfect pun.
Plain Jane: Brunettes Beware (*Harbinger Mystery, #1*) first published in 2010. It was also one of the first so-called eBooks that I had been made welcome to view, free of charge, in late December of 2012. And I had no sooner completed this title than an option to review it appeared on my screen, which, of course, I gladly did.
Unfortunately, my original review of *Plain Jane: Brunettes Beware* (*Harbinger Mystery, #1*)—which had been a more comprehensive analysis composed digitally rather than in longhand—was lost along with a small batch of other examinations I'd written in that same year. And this left me no other choice than to consult with any number of my handwritten notes.

While *Plain Jane: Brunettes Beware* (*Harbinger Mystery, #1*) is not one of the best dialogues of fiction I've ever read; nevertheless, it is a published work that had been offered to me by way of a complimentary copy, and it is deserving of my respect in that sense.

Pieced together from a few of those aforementioned handwritten notes, my brief critique of *Plain Jane: Brunettes Beware* (*Harbinger Mystery, #1*) is as follows:

TAKEN FROM THE WOMB.

Someone is murdering average-looking brunette women and removing their uteri to retain as trophies. And as a city becomes plunged in the depths of fear, detective Nicole Usher along with her partner—and former love interest—Ruben Torres, team up, even if grudgingly, with serial killer profiler Kent Harbinger—also a former love interest of detective Nicole Usher—to hunt down a vicious and elusive murderer.

Although the plot is quite intriguing at the outset—the opening premise will perhaps remind a few readers of *The Boston Strangler*—at some point, it begins to sputter. As it chugs along the tracks of its course, the narrative soon derails and becomes unbelievable. And if I've only one positive statement to utter concerning this effort, it is that I was able to obtain it free of charge.

Concerning *Plain Jane: Brunettes Beware* (*Harbinger Mystery, #1*), it is not a horrible read, only a very irritable one. And save for a few final words, I needn't go any further in my examination of it.

A FEW FINAL WORDS.

I will also mention that there was absolutely nothing, whatsoever, terrifying about this annoying work of serial killer fiction. Was it comparatively gross and obnoxious? Oh, most definitely. But was it *terrifying*? Did it live up to its '*Not for the faint of heart*' tagline? Well, only if someone is squeamish where human dismemberment and cannibalism are concerned.

To TKO me, a work of fiction would have to pack a powerful punch. And while she gave it her best shot, Cristyn West failed to blow me away with this one.

Whereas *Plain Jane: Brunettes Beware* (*Harbinger Mystery, #1*) had not been my cup of Tazo Passion, dear reader, it just may turn out to be one of the most riveting novels you've ever read. So be ye the judge.

Happy reading.

Cat Ellington's review of Killing Me Softly by Bianca Sloane

My rating: 5 out of 5 stars

Date read: January, 2013

THE SETUP.

Beautiful Chicago news producer, Tracy Ellis, has been brutally murdered along the icy shores of the city's famous lakefront. Many believe that the newlywed Ellis—a resident of Lakeview—was the misfortunate victim of an attempted mugging gone wrong. But was she? Was her grisly death the result of someone who coveted the contents of her wallet? Or was her heinous murder on that cold, wintry day the result of something (or someone) more sinister?

IN THE BEGINNING.

Documentary filmmaker Sondra Ellis—our leading lady, by the way—is back in Chicago to attend the Chicago Film Festival. Now living in New York, the California native does more than mingle with those of her fellow filmmakers; she also makes time to spend with her younger sister Tracy—the latter recently engaged to be married to Chicago pharmacist, Phillip Pearson.
The two lovebirds, especially Tracy, appear happy enough. And neither can wait until their big day. Despite having known one another for only a brief period, paradise eagerly intertwines with a whirlwind bliss. And both Phillip Pearson

and his gorgeous bride-to-be are surfing—non-stop—atop its perfect wave.

Indeed, all is joyful in the City of the Big Shoulders. And Sondra couldn't be happier for her little sister.

THE PROGRESSION OF TIME.

The entire Ellis clan is on hand for the big day, including Sondra and Tracy's famous parents, Gordon and Mimi. Gordon is an African-American professor at Stanford and best-selling author. And Mimi is a German-born former Olympic medalist swimmer turned swim coach.

Everything is exquisite. The bride, her groom, and even the sprawling Winnetka home—owned by Tracy's best friend Cicely Anderson, an award-winning anchorwoman in Chicago—at which Phillip Pearson takes Ms. Tracy Ellis to be his lawfully wedded wife.

More wowing is the fabulous honeymoon destination that awaits the eager newlyweds: glorious Jamaica.

Yes, everything is as smooth as peaches and cream. But as the old proverb states in its infinite wisdom: "The heart knows its own bitterness, and a stranger does not share its joy."

SHE'S NOT BETTER THAN ME!
IS SHE?

The worldly lot who star in this magnificent narrative go about their daily lives, immune to both the common and the unimportant alike.

Phillip, a carbon copy of Steve Urkel—according to the unspoken opinion of his new sister-in-law, Sondra—is away on a business trip, a pharmacy convention - while Tracy continues with her news career at home in Chicago. The newlyweds have a system that works well. And not a day passes without a phone call between them. In fact, on the day before her routine jog, Tracy and Phillip would chat (long-distance) about her plans for the fateful day, all of which would include stopping by the store for a few basic things on the way home. Chicago is expecting a snowstorm, and she can't be bothered to trek through it; it's best to get ahead of things. Her hubby, Phillip, totally agrees. And with that, their long-distance chat ends.

But Tracy Pearson, née Ellis, will never make it home.

For the face that had once been beautiful will soon be bludgeoned beyond recognition - as a horrifyingly wicked result of bitter envy, repugnant jealousy, and acidic hatred that a black-hearted murderer fostered towards the woman whose name had been Tracy Ellis Pearson.

TOO MANY UNANSWERED QUESTIONS.

What happened to Tracy Ellis Pearson on that arctic and dreadful day along Chicago's lakefront over one year ago? Her big sister, the chain-smoking Sondra—who would sooner gnaw off the beds of her fingernails than be deprived of a cigarette—is on a one-woman mission to find out. Something about the investigation into her sister's heinous murder doesn't sit well with her. And not content to accept her loss and move on, Sondra has now become a makeshift sleuth.
Too much time has passed without answers. And Sondra is not given a peaceful rest. Foremost in her thoughts is

her sister's widow, Phillip Pearson. Phillip had never been someone trustworthy as far as she was concerned, and it nipped at her that he seemed to be moving on so quickly in the aftermath of Tracy's death, er, murder. Naturally, Tracy's abrupt end is hard on everyone involved, especially Sondra and their parents. And between mourning the loss of her sister and trying to complete post-production work on her latest film, Sondra is several miles past famished.

Still, those pesky questions won't leave her be. And neither will that hidden anger.

Tracy was gone. And no one seemed to care outside of their immediate family. Famous parents or not, Tracy was a Black woman. And the world seemed to get over her senseless killing—in the world-class American city of Chicago—quick. Sure, her station ran coverage—if only for a little while—but overall, who cared?

Sondra desperately wants answers. And were it not for another glance at Tracy's obituary, she would never have gotten any.

NEW LIFE, NEW WIFE.

People die. And those of their loved ones who survive them must undergo the grieving process. It's only natural. But time heals all wounds. And eventually, life goes on.

Now situated in a suburban St. Louis village known as The Crossings, a quaint little subdivision of cul-de-sacs anchored by a gargantuan shopping and entertainment complex known as The Pavilion, Phillip Pearson has remarried and moved up a little bit higher in the world. Still the hardworking pharmacist, Phillip is at ease in his new life - as is he with his new wife, a lady named Paula. Way past mourning the death of his precious Tracy, Phillip is now happy again. And he only wishes to be left alone. Poor Phillip, he only wanted to leave all of his old pain behind him and move on. But the past has a way of awakening itself after a long slumber. It wakes up, gets in a good stretch, and goes about the business of pursuing those with whom it once had a history.

And in the case of Phillip Pearson, that history would include Sondra Ellis, a visitor to his new home - and a greeter of his frightfully submissive new wife.

Sondra Ellis. She should have just left well enough alone. But she just couldn't. Especially not after learning that Tracy had been planning to divorce the dubious Phillip Pearson.

But why? Had she not been happy? What didn't she reveal? Why did Phillip vacate Chicago? Did he know? Who else knew? And who the hell is Paula? This mysterious woman who will do any and everything in her power to be with Phillip?

A RABBIT HOLE OF MYSTERY, SUSPENSE, AND ANXIETY.

Devised in the vein of an old-era *Lifetime* movie, *Killing Me Softly*—Bianca Sloane's masterful debut in the fabled suspense thriller genre—guides the reader along one twisted path after another, gripping nerves and sending the emotions spinning like a top.

On the rapidly unfolding pages of this fabulous fiction, too many secrets go hand in hand with lies, deception, a hunger to control, and cold-blooded murder.

THE OTHER PLAYERS.

Added to an already superior company of top-billed personae are the following:

- Jack Turner, Tracy's ex-boyfriend and a successful restaurateur in Chicago

- Gary Tate, Sondra's ex-husband who is all things, including wealthy, alluring, and a drunkard

- Damon Randall, Tracy's divorce attorney

- Cindy Cross, Phillip and Paula's new—and notoriously nosy—neighbor

- Miss Mira, neighbor to Phillip and Paula, a new buddy to Cindy Cross, and a shameless gossiper

- Carlene, Paula's flamboyant hairstylist

- Detective Marion Wallace, the lead investigator assigned to work the Tracy Ellis cold case and this effort's "Olivia Benson"

- Kevin Henderson, a native South Sider, a social worker for the Chicago Public Schools system, one who is most deceptive and covetous and Phillip Pearson's old buddy from their college days at UIC

- Dr. Don Keegan, psychiatrist, business associate to Phillip Pearson, prescription drug addict, and white-collar criminal

- Maxine, second-in-command staff pharmacist at Phillip's clinic and unwitting pawn

PRAISE FOR THE AUTHOR.

Graced with vision and an admirable knack for storytelling, Bianca Sloane presents a new style. She brings depth to the inimitable thriller genre. And this is evident as her exciting debut, *Killing Me Softly*, so optimistically proves. It was an honor to make the acquaintance of her well-written - and generously recommended - literature by way of a complimentary copy. And that declaration will forever stand with me.

Five lowdown-dirty-and-shameful stars.

Cat Ellington's review of The Butterfly Killer (The Driving Lesson) by Charles W. Harvey

My rating: 5 out of 5 stars

Date read: February, 2013

DON'T DREAM IT'S OVER.

Whenever you complete a work of fiction, and the premise of its dialogue lingers on your psyche, even into the next day, then it would be safe to say that such a narrative was well-written in its presentation. Such is the case with the disturbing tale currently under review: *The Butterfly Killer (The Driving Lesson)* - authored by the talented Charles W. Harvey.

Maniacal and bone-chilling, Harvey's *The Butterfly Killer (The Driving Lesson)* acquaints the reader with one Mr. Elliott Cross, a man who thinks that by murdering those who dare to dream, he renders a justifiable service to the living God, even Jehovah himself.
For according to the twisted doctrines of Elliott Cross, those who dare to dream dishonor Father God, what by having their aspirations—as though the same were false idols—before a trembling fear of Him. You see, this is the perverse mindset of the man named Elliott Cross – a driving instructor, by the way. As Elliott Cross sees it, those who dream are not worthy of life. And that would include the young man named Timmy, his daughter Carrie's good friend.

Timmy's dream is like that of most of his fellow teens: he wants to pass his driver's test and procure his very first driver's license. Nothing wrong with that. Right? Oh, you bet there is.

Timmy would love to share the news of his progress (thanks to an extra lesson) with Carrie, but Mr. Elliott Cross doesn't believe that idea to be so wise. 'She'll only be jealous,' Mr. Cross says. 'Your friends will be as mad as wet hens!' Mr. Cross says.

Mr. Elliott Cross? He hates dreamers.

AN EERIE FOOTNOTE.

For a thriller of only twelve pages, *The Butterfly Killer* (*The Driving Lesson*) is quite creepy in spirit. And it will completely absorb the reader deep into the warped mind of a ruthless murderer who projects—and quite well, I might add—the genteel disposition of an all-American, suburban dad.

Vehemently recommended to those enthusiasts of suspense thrillers, *The Butterfly Killer* (*The Driving Lesson*) is a fiction of not only gripping apprehension but also a perfect little read for a wet and dreary day.

Five fluttering stars.

Cat Ellington's review of Status by Jordan Belcher

My rating: 5 out of 5 stars

Date read: March, 2013

ERRBODY AIN'T CHO FRIEND.

Be careful of those from whom you accept friend requests on social media.

A menacing and suspenseful urban thriller, *Status*—set in Kansas City, Missouri—orbits around a sensational African-American ensemble led by a beautiful twenty-two-year-old fitness instructor named Tyesha Fenty. The mother of a five-year-old daughter named Kylie Brown, Tyesha is not unlike any other Millennial where social media is concerned. She engages in all the things that go along with the flow of the social media community. And like several others, she is often tempted to share too many details about her personal life with strangers who only serve to pose as familiar persons.

Sure, there are plenty of insecure people out there in the world who desperately depend on Likes, Loves, Comments, or Retweets to act as self-esteem and self-worth validators. But there are also many other individuals, of the secure and self-confident lot, who are at ease to enjoy the original purpose of social media in the first place: connecting with others, particularly those who constitute the thread of their genuinely familiar friends and family.

Unfortunately, the latter cannot be applied here. For with false friends like those cast members of the scandalous and vile tale currently under review, who in the hell needs enemies?

ADD FRIEND.

It's just another day on The Site, the world's largest—and most popular—social network. Many folks, both well-known and unknown, are scrolling through their news feeds, subscribing to public pages, following other users, posting photos and captions, liking, commenting, and talking loud and saying absolutely nothing.
It's the ultimate hangout spot, The Site. And Tyesha Fenty, along with various members of her online network, lays snuggled beneath the heavy quilt of the platform's digital confines.
Indeed, The Site has become an obsession for many. And the bootylicious Tyesha Fenty has become an obsession but for only one.

On the day Tyesha Fenty accepted that friend request from someone connected to someone else in her network, she could not have known that it would mark the beginning of her worst nightmare.

HOES, THUGS, COMPETITORS, AND KILLERS.

Tyesha is young and long-suffering. Sometimes wise, other times gullible, Tyesha Fenty continues to hold out hope that one day Rodrick Brown—otherwise known as Rodrick Al-Bashir—will finally pop the question. But no can do for Mr. Brown. Because you see, the streets? They keep calling his name. The thug life? It keeps calling his name. Violence towards his competitors? It keeps calling his name. Loose, around-the-way women who desperately covet his long con hustle? Well, they're not only calling his name, but they're also going so far as to consistently comment on his posts on The Site—right before the prying eyes of baby mama, Tyesha.

For these loose, around-the-way women are without shame, wells without water, clouds carried by a tempest: street tramps. And learning but never coming to a knowledge of the truth, Rodrick Brown, a double-minded man who is unstable in *all* his ways, continues to fall prey to such.

But lurking in the wings is another who watches closely, observing every action and inaction. One who is none too pleased with the mistreatment of Tyesha Fenty. One who wants her beauty and her soft curvaceousness all to himself. And he'll do right by her and Kylie, too. He won't dog her out or take her for granted like that arrogant asshole, Rodrick.

Matter of fact, he just may have to do away with that nigga—and any other muthafucka in his way—if that'll get him to Tyesha.

For now, though, just hang back and holla at her on The Site. And follow her around K-town. Sooner or later, some'n gon' break. A whole lotta these muthafuckas gon' break.

THE CAST.

Neutralized by an indelible company of supporting players, *Status* is an engrossing masterwork of urban fiction meritable of only the most-noble reverence in its respective class.

The men and women who co-star in this raucous drama are none other than the awesomely gifted following:

- Quita Wheeler, a pathetic sinner, a side chick to Rodrick Brown, and a snake in the grass

- Gideon Byers, a close friend to Rodrick, a kind and respectful helper to many, and a pathological liar

- Velma Fenty, a cordial mother to Tyesha, a tolerable grandmother to Kylie, and a hateful bitch with many family secrets

- Kenneth Murberry, a long-time enemy and archrival to Rodrick Brown and the significant other to the unfaithful Wendy Hartley—a triflin' broad who serves her crooked purpose on these pages as not only a scheming baby mama to Kenneth but also a disgusting side ho' to Rodrick

While Belcher incorporates more bit players and extras in his first-rate troupe, including Angela Serrano and Joanne Dunley, the gifted author outdoes himself with the scalding introduction of Deja Michelle - a trusted confidante and best friend to Tyesha since high school.

Formerly overweight, Deja Michelle now flaunts a figure eight and a smiling face that is truly anything but joy-induced: for the eyes implanted within her lovely face toil long and hard to conceal the truth that lies deep within her soul. A soul intoxicated by the fumes of an embittered, murderous rage.

SUMMARIZING THE URBAN EXPERIENCE.

Social media news feeds, status updates, lies, false faces, hatred, revenge, envy, jealousy, malice, anger, gullibility, non-stop sex, stalking, and murder: they all come together in a cutthroat effort to destroy the very lives - and souls - of every man, woman, and child involved on these suspenseful and ghetto-fabulous pages.
For whithersoever the stars of this fiction venture, the foot-shuffling drama is sure to follow.

WORTHY OF A STANDING OVATION.

Incredible is the literary vision of Jordan Belcher, and exquisite is his written composition.
Status, now listed as one of my all-time favorite works in urban fiction, absolutely refused to allow me time to sleep. For it preoccupied my reader even into the wee hours. And I will never forget my experience with it.

While I eagerly recommend *Status* to those fellow readers who, like myself, lust for splendid thrillers in the urban fiction genre, I thank Felony Books for its kind gesture of offering *Status* to the literary community by way of complimentary copies.
Kudos, Jordan Belcher: for your creative impression forever memorable.

Five stealthy-and-obsessive stars.

Chapter 3
Getting the Hang of It

Cat Ellington's review of Big Girls Do It Better (Big Girls Do It #1) by Jasinda Wilder

My rating: 5 out of 5 stars

Date read: July, 2013

"Torn between two lovers, feelin' like a fool—
Lovin' both of you is breakin' all the rules"
—Mary MacGregor, *Torn Between Two Lovers* (1976)

THE DIVINE MISS ANNA.

According to her mother, Anna Devine has always been fat, even as a child. And Anna's answer to that? Passion. Anna has a passion for life that translates into a bit of overindulgence, and she makes no apologies for it. She loves food. Anna Devine loves to eat, especially sweets. Hey, give her a crème brûlée or a perfectly moist cupcake on any given day, and she'll devour them whole like a real boss. As one might guess, Anna Devine also has an insatiable appetite for the art of lovemaking.

WHAT DID THE DOCTOR SAY?

Maybe that's why our leading lady, Anna, can never seem to get enough of either. And when she finds herself entangled in a fiery love triangle with two of the hottest men in town—one of whom just so happens to be a rising rock star—testosterone levels will explode. Indeed, masculine genitals will harden themselves in compliance, and her swollen (and drenched) vulva will be stretched wide open, even beyond what she could have ever imagined.

Indeed, her mother was right.
Anna Devine is a big girl. And she can take it.

CHASE OR JEFF? JEFF OR CHASE?

Oh, dear! Two attractive men in Chase Delany and Jeff Cartwright, only one beautifully sexy Anna Devine. But there's enough of her to go around for sure.

Anna has just finished her shift at a bar called The Dive, where she works alongside her business partner, Jeff, as the house DJ. Craving a sweet treat, she wanders over to the late-night eatery, Ram's Horn, to grab a bite—a slice of lemon pie—and bumps into the tall, dark and handsome Chase Delany, a so-called "rock god" in the making. Making pleasantries more lively, Anna apologizes for her clumsiness, and the two begin to converse, eventually moseying their way around to name introductions. And before long, the ample Anna creates her very own moniker for Chase Delany: Mr. Sexypants.
It works, what this private new nickname that he has absolutely no idea exists. And before long, the ample Anna is on her knees—outside behind the restaurant—serving the hot rocker her most divine oral pleasure.

Her name is Devine - for a reason. And she wants to wow Chase Delany forever. Of course, it wouldn't hurt much if he felt the same way, which he does. Chase is blown away—literally—by Anna. And he only wants to wow her forever. Forever and ever.

Imagine that, what a fling saturated with an ejaculation of lust. Oh, yes, it all would be rather sensual - except for one big and beefy problem. Jeff Cartwright.

Whereas Chase Delany is a rock star riding the escalator up to the clouds of international fame, Jeff Cartwright—just as tall and good-looking as Chase—is simply the kind of ordinary average guy that Joe Walsh sings about in his classic song.

Jeff sings, too. He has a tremendous voice, knocking 'em dead at The Dive whenever he and his fantasy girl, Anna, team up to perform as a duo on the bar stage before their adoring patrons. Sure, they click as business partners, Jeff and Anna, but Jeff wants more. He wants to take their relationship to the next level, but Anna? She can't go there. At least not right now, not with Chase dominating her every thought. She has feelings for Jeff, of course, she does, but she can't shake her obsession with Chase. With Jeff, her emotions are a factor, but with Chase? Well, with Chase, her sexual needs command instant gratification. With Chase, she can lose control and be all of those things she has never been: sexually desired and a beautiful goddess. But with Jeff, she is forced to be grounded and focused, and in control. And God knows she needs the former just as much as she does the latter.

Both of these men want—and need—her. And Anna needs them. They both love her, and *she* loves them.
What to do? What to do?
Oh, dear. Oh, dear.

What a dramatic dilemma in which Anna Devine has moaned and hissed herself. How will she ever be able to choose one man over the other? How did she ever get herself caught in the middle of this tug-of-war of steamy love with two men pulling her from one end to the other? And how could he ask her to marry him at a time like this?

Oh, dear Anna. Oh, dear, sweet Anna.
He wants you so badly that he's willing to battle fist and fury.

COOLING DOWN AFTER A HOT CLIMAX.

What a spectacular tale we've ourselves in *Big Girls Do It Better* (*Big Girls Do It, #1*)! The first release in a series of erotic fascination, *Big Girls Do It Better* (*Big Girls Do It, #1*) was my exciting introduction to its author, Jasinda Wilder, and I've been one of her most admiring fans ever since. Excellent dialogue!

Co-starring the unlucky-in-love Jamie, who sparkles on these fleeting pages as Anna's (thinner) best friend and roommate, *Big Girls Do It Better* (*Big Girls Do It, #1*) does sublime justice to its respective classification of erotica. And the novella is way past worthy of my reviewer's most enthusiastic recommendation.

Great work, Jasinda Wilder. I look forward to completing this succession as I am dying to know what happens next. Oh, dear.

Five eeny-meeny-miny-moe stars.

Cat Ellington's review of Why Me? (A Date to Die For #1) by Bonnie R. Paulson

My rating: 5 out of 5 stars

Date read: August, 2013

REMINISCING.

Yet another member of my lost files, *Why Me? (A Date to Die For #1)* had been among an intriguing set of eBooks that I'd read after conjoining myself with the Internet Sphere in 2012.

During the following year of 2013, I received the novella under review as a complimentary copy courtesy of *Barnes & Noble*. And though I'd composed a brief review of the dialogue no sooner than I'd concluded it at that time, I regret to inform you, dear reader, that I am unable to retrieve said review today – despite my extensive search efforts. Therefore I must—for the sake of recognizing this chilling novelette as one that I'd so enjoyed the tremendous pleasure of reading at the outset of its release—render the fleeting tale the literary examination due it, even if by way of old notes.

My original commencement and summary of this psychological thriller will feature as follows:

DATING IN THE NEW MILLENNIUM.

The plot rotates around our attractive leading lady, Molly, who finally agrees to go on a first date with a very handsome, albeit unrelenting, man at the urging of her two best friends. They want to see Molly get back into life after the sudden loss of her identical twin sister. Molly suspects that her suspicious death may or may not have been the result of murder. So to take her mind off things, the two women turn her onto a popular speed dating site specialized in mingling singles. Everything seems fine with the service during the initial stages. But then again, some things (and some people) always do.

A certain handsome man who would perhaps be considered the dreamboat of every gal engaged in fantasy is the same man with whom Molly makes a very clumsy connection. But what lies beneath the surface of his handsome countenance is something more than just his genetic dermis. It is something else downright disturbing - and wholly sinister.

Perhaps it would have been better if Molly had remained, well, you know, a mingling single.

A HARD TO FIND CLASSIC.

Composed of only 31 pages, *Why Me? (A Date to Die For #1)* is a read that I greatly recommend, that is, if you can locate it. For where it had been widely available in 2013, today, it is a difficult book to come by. And that is the only regret I have concerning it.

Thank you, Bonnie R. Paulson, for the gift that is Book One in this series. Many women will relate to this storyline. And I enjoyed it tremendously.
Kudos!

Five dangerously troubled stars.

Cat Ellington's review of 3:00 AM (Henry Bins #1) by Nick Pirog

My rating: 5 out of 5 stars

Date read: October, 2013

"One hour. Sixty minutes. Three thousand, six hundred seconds. That's how long I get each day. How long I'm awake."
—NIGHTOWL3AM

THERE'S A HEART OF A NIGHT OWL CALLIN'.

This wonderfully unique and comfortably quiet thriller is one with which I will always be in love. Another addition to my brand-new eLibrary in 2013, *3:00 AM* (*Henry Bins #1*) is a plot that orbits around thirty-six-year-old Henry Bins, our leading man. Henry Bins is suffering from—or living with—an isolated medical condition known as Henry Bins Syndrome. Named for Henry, this rare disease is a debilitating sleep disorder that causes those affected by it to sleep twenty-three hours a day, affording them only one full hour of awake time before sleep returns to seize them all over again.

For Henry Bins, his waking hour spans from 3:00 A.M. to 4:00 A.M., during which time he reads books—a few pages at a time—on his *Kindle*, eats meals, and drinks the protein shakes that are generously prepared for him by his beloved housekeeper, Isabel. Henry also uses this time to check out his lucrative stocks on the stock market, to play

Game of Thrones in spurts, and to get in a quick run before finally winding down with a hot shower in preparation for his long sleep pattern ahead. A long sleep pattern that pulls him back into automatic slumber mode like clockwork every twenty-three hours on the dot.

That's life for the lovable Henry Bins.
And it's about to throw him for one helluva mysterious loop-the-loop.

SHE'S CRYIN' IN THE NIGHT.

On one fateful morning, while returning home to his Washington, DC area condo from his wee-hour run, the nocturnal Henry witnesses a car pulling into the driveway of one of his neighbors across the street but thinks nothing of it. Minding his own business, he continues onward, home.

Now safe inside of his condo, Henry Bins, still with about a minute to spare before his body falls into its deep sleep, hears the piercing scream of a woman coming from somewhere outside, an audible echo in the dead of night. Henry goes to look from his window. And he immediately knows the source from which the scream came: the neighbor's house across the street. It is the same house into whose driveway the mysterious car had just pulled. Henry, with only seconds left, sights a man emerging from the woman's home. Someone has murdered her. And right before sleep arrives to claim him for the next twenty-three hours, Henry can make out the man's face beneath the streetlight. While checking his surroundings, the man instinctively looks up. And both he and Henry lock eyes.

Two seconds before he falls into his diurnal sleep, Henry recognizes the man. The man is the President of the United States.

ADRENALINE, ANYONE?

From there, folks, we have ourselves a bona fide winner in *3:00 AM (Henry Bins #1)*! With fleeting pagination of only 100, *3:00 AM (Henry Bins #1)* is an electrifying page-turner that packs one solid punch after another, rope-a-doping the reader's psyche with a pummeling of iron-fisted suspense. Nick Pirog's *3:00 AM (Henry Bins #1)* is one of the best novellas of its time. And I am supremely honored to say that said work still makes itself at home in the cozy confines of my massive digital library. Expect to be awake into the wee hours—pun intended—with this one. For it is just that fascinating of a read, indeed.

Five dead-to-the-world stars.

Cat Ellington's review of Boy Next Door – The First 11 Days by Emma Clark

My rating: 4 out of 5 stars

Date read: January, 2014

HEY GIRL, MOVE A LITTLE CLOSER.

The boy meets the girl. The girl is immediately attracted to the tall, dark, and handsome boy. The boy wants to buy the girl a coffee. And the girl gladly accepts. The boy starts to lay on his boyish charm, and the girl gushes and blushes in response. The girl has car trouble, and the boy offers the girl a ride as a courtesy. The girl happily accepts. The boy keeps on the boyish charm until he can get the girl into his car. The girl is ultimately unwary and haplessly needy. The boy is eerily sadistic and treacherously wicked.

Meet Brandon Levine, Mia's most horrifying nightmare - and her most delectable desire.

DOMINATED BY AN ALPHA MALE.

Set in Houston, *Boy Next Door – The First 11 Days* is any and everything but kindly. The extremely-short introduction to the *Boy Next Door* series is downright atrocious and repulsively unsettling.

Where Brandon and Mia are concerned, "Christian Grey" and "Anastasia Steele" pale, shamefully, in comparison. And you, dear reader, will be further convinced after you've spent eleven days locked away in a secret hideaway with a madman who has become the BND master to your submissive sex slave.

Dare you try to escape—especially when you don't even know where you are.

LUST NOT, WANT NOT.

A 45-minute read guaranteed to wreak havoc on the viewer's psyche, *Boy Next Door – The First 11 Days* only serves to prove that old, timeless adage: 'Everything that looks good ain't good for you.'

Emma Clark does a fine job with her storyline on these pages. And if you are one of those people that fancies only the kinkiest of Bondage and Domination erotica, consider the tale presently under review highly recommended. However, if such content is a novice to you, I would only advise that you approach this particular narrative with caution.

Enjoy the pleasure.

Cat Ellington's review of The Duke's Guide to Correct Behavior (Dukes Behaving Badly, #1) by Megan Frampton

My rating: 2 out of 5 stars

Date read: December, 2014

OH, HEAVENS, I DO SAY.

I have read many Victorian romance novels in my time. And they can always be wagered on to guarantee the following attributes: a beautiful, sassy, supple, and young virgin maiden; a tall, tanned and muscular Lord, Duke, or Count, whom, by the way, will be destined to fall helpless victim to the captivating charms of the lady-in-waiting; bottomless wells of jaw-dropping wealth and riches; sprawling manors; endless drama between both the Noble and the maiden, etc.

And on the pages of Megan Frampton's *The Duke's Guide to Correct Behavior (Dukes Behaving Badly, #1)*, such a premise is no different.

Misunderstand me not, dear reader. I love a good romance novel. But the dialogue presently under review didn't excite me in the same way that other fictional works of a similar class had in so many years prior. And because of that, I am inclined not to render it my most gracious applause. However, you may find it to your liking, and therefore should consider the effort respectfully recommended.

While I believe that such commonality in the storylines of this genre has waxed itself weary; nevertheless, there will forever remain an audience for its perfect fantasy. And this is something that no one, not even myself, can put asunder.

Happy reading.

Chapter 4
Slowly But Surely

Cat Ellington's review of Selfie (Status Book 4) by Jordan Belcher

My rating: 5 out of 5 stars

Date read: March, 2015

"A man *of* great wrath will suffer punishment; for if you rescue *him*, you will have to do it again."
—Proverbs 19:19

LET'S GO CRAZY.

With *Selfie (Status Book 4)*, the genius of its authorship, Jordan Belcher, continues to reiterate itself to those of his readers in a most resplendent fashion: for it is simply not content to be denied.

This outstanding thriller transports the viewer to Kansas City, Missouri - where we come to make the acquaintance of 24-year-old Renae Watson, the Audi-driving, ultra-feminine, delicate, and gorgeous career woman who just so happens to be engaged to one of the most successful attorneys in the state. Like many of those in her respective age group, Renae Watson spends a significant amount of time on her social media profiles, especially on

The Site, where her extended circle of *"friends"* includes Tyesha Fenty and Rodrick Brown, the stars of Belcher's *Status* trilogy.

THE CALM BEFORE THE STORM.

Renae Watson is pretty much at peace in her life. She's between jobs, but she has her Church, her fabulous car, her enviable wardrobe, and, of course, Christian Kundert, her 39-year-old Caucasian beau. She does well and would be at liberty to enjoy her life were it not for her troubled cousin, Lataya Farroll.

Due to strong family genetics, Lataya Farroll is practically the spitting image of her better off cousin, Renae. And because the women are the same age (and were raised) together, their relationship is extremely close-knit. The girls do nearly everything together. And there couldn't be a twosome of cuzzos more kindred in spirit than they.

But the conflict that keeps rearing its ugly head between this unusual duo of women is Lataya's personality compared to that of Renae. While Renae is upstanding, law-abiding, hardworking, and somewhat God-fearing, Lataya is ruthless, gangsta, violent, street-taught, and chronically unemployed. So much alike, yet so different, are these two. And because Renae must clean up after Lataya whenever the latter incites chaos—which is often—her patience, not to mention her sanity, is beginning to wear thin. Renae knows that Lataya's recklessness can—and will—lead to her doom if she fails to cut the troubled soul loose. But how can she? Lataya is family. And she needs her.

Renae is all Lataya has. And Renae knows this. So, for now, she, Renae, has no other choice but to remain in her role as the human pacifier. For as long as she does, all will remain peaceful.

MAIN CHICKS VS. SIDE CHICKS.

Ladies? If you ever have to fight with another woman to secure a place on the right arm of any man, know for a certainty that the same is not the man for you. Because if he were, there would be no need for you to do battle with another woman in a strenuous effort to defend your position in his life.
Here is where wisdom cries aloud to those whose ears are open, that they should hear her: for a real man will play the man. A real man will not allow himself to fall under the spell of temptation beyond what is moral and justified. A real man will declare the woman for whom his passion is. And that declaration alone would invoke a strong enough rebuke to chase away any skanky homewreckers at heart.

Bret Hustler has been a very naughty boy of late, cheating on the aggressively jealous, insecure, and crazy Lataya with her worst enemy, Talia Price. Blatant in his infidelity, Bret Hustler has not made the pretty (and wildly popular) Talia a secret to anyone except Lataya. But now, Lataya knows, and so does Renae. And the vicious mocking (from others) has gotten itself underway on The Site.
One status update after another is full of hateful barbs, insults, vindictiveness, and ridicule from the troubled main chick to the instigating side chick.
Indeed, Bret Hustler, together with the roving eye of his penis, has brought about a blackened atmosphere of striving on the popular social media platform—onto which

many have settled themselves—that adds more fuel to an already kindled fire.

As expected, Bret Hustler—an individual true to his name—is in complete and utter denial, refusing to man-up, and further infuriating his main chick, the dangerously volatile Lataya.
On and on it goes, the triangle of lust. Until one of them winds up murdered.

From there, Old Scratch makes his otherworldly entrance, that he may lay claim on those given to him to sift like wheat. For he has asked. And to him, it has been granted.

THE BREAKDOWN.

One of the most captivating narratives in its maniacal class is Jordan Belcher's *Selfie* (*Status Book 4*). The effort is a magnificently enjoyable tale saturated in a corrosive culture of social media – where one's *"friends"* are not their friends; and where deception, envy, jealousy, and many lies hover over the heads of those unsuspecting.
Selfie continues the drama and madness of its equally superior predecessors, *Status, Status 2,* and *Status 3*—combining just the right amount of thrills, mystery, and suspense to keep the reader on edge from start to finish.

While Renae Watson is flawless in her performance as this effort's leading lady battling a legion of old demons, she is flanked by a supporting cast nothing short of outstanding, including:

- Leon Staples, a popular (but physically abusive) Site friend and Lataya's other lover on the down-low (or low down, if you will)

- Dante Barber, a semi-popular user on The Site, a chocolate-hued party promoter with six-pack abs, and the man of Renae Watson's soaking wet dreams

- Benny Dobbs, a big-time prosecutor and an associate of Christian Kundert

- Detectives Copeland and Frisk, partners at the helm of the murder investigation

However small and compact, this talented troupe of supporting players is only made better by a strong unit of ghetto-bred key bit players and extras who play their roles to perfection on the world's largest social network.

Despite being only a tad bit slower (in pace) than its trilogy of antecedents, *Selfie* (*Status Book 4*) boasts tremendous detail and thorough research where it pertains to the field of psychiatry. It is a fascinating script, and I will not neglect to render it my loftiest recommendation.
Once again, Jordan Belcher's literary vision has wowed my reader to the majestic level of unfaltering admiration. And I applaud him wholeheartedly.

Five dissociative stars.

Cat Ellington's review of Status 2 by Jordan Belcher

My rating: 5 out of 5 stars

Date read: April, 2015

RELATIONSHIP STATUS: IT'S COMPLICATED.

SIX MONTHS LATER – The script to Jordan Belcher's *Status 2* dramatically picks up where *Status*, book one in the Status Trilogy, left off. Rodrick Brown—a man always learning but never able to come to a knowledge of the truth—is being released from the Moberly Correctional Facility (or prison, if you like) for crimes committed six months earlier. And awaiting him on the other side of the maximum-security gate is our long-suffering leading lady Tyesha Fenty - along with their five-year-old daughter, Kylie.

After the horrific nightmare that unfolded in all of their lives only a few short months ago, coupled with Rodrick's chronic infidelity, Tyesha has made it up in her mind to heal as both a single woman and a single mother. She is through with the drama.
Or so she thinks.

Unbeknownst to the arrogant and hypocritical Rodrick, Tyesha has been seeing someone else during his brief time on lockdown. Marley DuBois.

Assigned the username *"Fedbound Marley"* on the ever-popular social media platform, The Site, Marley

DuBois has all but moved in with Tyesha and Kylie - and taken Rodrick's place. And while Tyesha has convinced herself that she and Marley are only "Site friends," are they? You know, only friends?
See, Marley doesn't know that Tyesha has invited Rodrick to live with her and Kylie.

Marley also doesn't know that Rodrick has just dropped to one knee and proposed marriage to Tyesha—right outside the barbed wire gates of Moberly Correctional Facility.

UNLEASH THE DRAMA.

The Site is an obsession for this effort's hard-minded cast: they all spend every waking hour of the day scrolling their news feeds, posting status updates, Liking status updates, commenting on the status updates of their so-called friends, willing their Site notification ringtones to sound, and acting as busybodies in the affairs—both the literal and figurative ones—of others.
And Tyesha Fenty, despite her air of self-righteousness, ain't no different.

Social media can be as powerfully addictive as any given narcotic; and on the fast-paced pages of this immoral sequel to *Status*, the same is also likely to be just as deadly.

BITTER ENEMIES.

Rodrick Brown can't wait to get back in the sack under Tyesha's roof. But what he cannot even begin to understand is that Tyesha has invited her mother—the callous, vindictive, ruthless, and notorious Velma Fenty—to live with her after Velma suffered a foreclosure on her own quaint home not so long ago.

Indeed, much has changed since his incarceration. But this setup is by far the worst change that could ever occur because Rodrick hates Velma Fenty from the furthest depths of his soul. And Velma hates Rodrick Brown from the furthest depths of hers.

As it is written: "Better is a dry morsel with quietness than a house full of feasting with strife."

UNHINGE THE MADNESS.

Tyesha Fenty has accomplished a few things since we first met her in book one, including a promotion at work (she's now the Supervisor of the Kansas City DMV), her own home, and a nice little nest egg of savings. Her focus is admirable, but her inability to liberate herself from Rodrick Brown and all of the drama associated with him isn't.

Case in point: Dava Babcock. Dava Babcock is pregnant with Rodrick's second child—a boy at that. And Dava Babcock loves to gush and gloat in her status updates about the unborn *Rodrick, Jr.*

Of course, the purpose of it all is to trouble Tyesha. Because Dava Babcock *knows* that baby mama number one cannot resist reading her status updates, especially where they pertain to her pregnancy with Rodrick's second child—a boy at that.

Dava envies Tyesha, as do so many others whose smiles disguise the truth of their spirits. And she desires to see Tyesha come undone emotionally. That's just the spiteful nature of the side chick. It's universal. But somewhere hidden amid this ridiculously-animated bunch is another Site friend who feels the need to protect Tyesha from the likes of her enemies.

A different kind of murderous stalker, this individual has slithered in undetected. And those who have their minds are filled up with the cares of the world will never see the scythe of death coming.

THE TROUBLE SEEKERS.

Marley DuBois likes the perception that people have of him: an upstanding brotha on the straight and narrow. But it is what it is: a *perception*.

Marley DuBois is all about his hustle, too. Only he's not as good at the dirty street game as Rodrick. And his best friend, Deven Torres—the man with whom Marley rips and runs and does evil—is not as good at the dirty street game as Skooly, Rodrick's best bud. And while swaggering along the dark and dusky sidewalks of their self-destructive lives, these four men will cross paths in the most terrifying of ways. Rodrick and Marley both feel that they have much to prove as men, particularly where it pertains to the hairy genitals of Tyesha Fenty. And the two rivals commence to battle it out on The Site by way of insulting tags directed at one another via status updates.

Moreover, their petty feud intensifies after a photo of Tyesha sitting in Marley's lap goes viral.

DID YOU GET MY LETTER?

Just when Tyesha Fenty thought it was safe to get her groove back in life after the horrible ordeal that both she

and her daughter had to survive on the vicious pages of *Status*, she receives the first letter containing three blood-curdling words:
Watch your back.

The spirit of the written words is most hostile. And the callous scribbler succeeds at instilling fear in the mind of Tyesha Fenty.
To make matters worse, Kylie—the dearest heart of her frightened mother—has gone missing - without a trace.

THE NETWORK.

Evident of superior casting is the undeniably gifted ensemble of bit players who fabulously complement our chief performers throughout this script, including:

- Landon "*LadyKiller*" Fenty, Tyesha's long-lost—and profoundly beloved—brother and Site friend

- Kayla and Kendal Fenty, Landon's adorable daughters

- Journie DuBois, Marley's 57-year-old aunt - and Site friend

- Joanne Dunley, DMV co-worker to Tyesha and Site Friend

- Christina "*MsFineGirl*," a great votary of Tyesha and Site friend

- Rita "*RealSpit*" Gibson, a true-blue sweetheart and Site friend

- Angela "*youngandfly*" Serrano, another loose feather in the "Jimmy Hat" of Rodrick Brown and Site friend

- Janice Tillot, a forever concerned Site friend

- Deja Michelle, a ghost from the past and wannabe Site friend

- Kenneth "*C.r.e.a.m.*" Murberry and Edward Young, real niggas and Site friends

- Harold the Moneyman, Julius Taylor, Michael "*StreetLawyer*," and VVS Vernon, four bona fide instigators - and ghetto-minded Site friends

- Mitch "*tiredofballin*" Walker, Smitty "*Down4Whatever*," Monica "*I'mProbably*" Wright, and Wendy "*youlovetotaste*" Hartley, drama enthusiasts and just another triflin' bundle of ghetto-minded Site friends

Know for a certainty that as the sun sets itself down at eve, a good night's rest will make haste to elude those listed above.

A SOPHOMORE SUCCESS.

With a few more squirts of Sriracha added to an already heated plot of deceit, dread, revenge, murder, and suspense, Detectives Copeland, Frisk, and Rosan of the Kansas City P.D. co-star in this masterwork as the lead officials investigating a string of murders, arson, and possible kidnapping.

Following its masterful predecessor, *Status*, *Status 2* will by no means bore its reader - not even a teeny bit.
A tale that I would gladly recommend to anyone in the literary community, particularly those who make up its urban thriller block, *Status 2* has earned a place in the top ranks as one of my all-time favorite works of fiction. And I will forever foster a genuine respect for its incredible authorship.

For as *Jaws* made you afraid to go out in the water, and *Psycho* made you afraid to take showers, so will Jordan Belcher's *Status 2* make you afraid to accept friend requests on any given social media platform.

Five miserably perturbed stars.

Cat Ellington's review of The Organ Takers: A Novel of Surgical Suspense (The McBride Trilogy Book 1) by Richard Van Anderson

My rating: 5 out of 5 stars

Date read: May, 2015

ARE YOU AN ORGAN DONOR?

Michael Smith, a paranoid schizophrenic all alone in the world, awakens to find himself deep in the throat of a cold, dark alley in midtown Manhattan. He can't remember how he got there, only that he's in a lot of pain now. It's January. Michael knows this. And it's bitter-cold outside; his hands are freezing. Michael thinks back, back to the place where he had last been. His memory is somewhat foggy, but it doesn't fail him completely. He can remember—ouch! The pain is unbearable - like someone slashed him with a razor-sharp scalpel and left him to bleed out. But he's still alive. *Thank God.* Michael tries to remember.

People were working on me. Yeah. People were working on me; they were wearing coverings over their faces. And I was lying on an operating table.

Oh, dear God, the pain is excruciating. Michael lifts his shirt to check his side, the source of his fiery pain. There's no blood, only soft gauze. But what lies beneath that gauze will petrify him beyond what is comprehensible. His skin stapled - starting at his side and disappearing behind his back. He has been operated on, but by whom? Who has done this horrible thing to him?

Was it the electric company? Yes, perhaps it was the electric company because they've been after me for a while now.

Michael thinks. He wonders what happened to him.

It was the electric company. It was the electric company. I have to get out of this alley, but I can hardly move - so much pain. I have to make it out of this cold, dark alley. Somebody help me!

Those would be the final thoughts of the violently desecrated Michael Smith.

THE LAWLESS AND THE DEPRAVED.

Dr. Andrew Turnbull is a megalomaniac who also happens to be depraved and perverse. Dr. Andrew Turnbull is the founder of the NuLife Corporation. And he only has a few goals that he would like to reach in his godless life. They include appeasing Mr. White, obtaining the love of the world, and winning medicine's most prestigious honor, the Nobel Peace Prize.

Mr. White—the NSA spook in whose debt Dr. Andrew Turnbull is so embedded—is a man who remains to be seen, except by those who are at will to do his hideous bidding, including Dr. Andrew Turnbull.
A shameful flunkie for the shockingly powerful Mr. White, Dr. Andrew Turnbull would, but, for only a piece of bread,

transgress – even if it means that he must kill in the process.

On the pages of this appalling—albeit nimbly-written—medical thriller, we come to make the acquaintance of those both good and evil. And David McBride, a disgraced but gifted surgeon—who also happens to be our leading man—is to be counted among the former.

PRESSURE.

Blacklisted from the surgical branch of medicine, the result of certain "ethical violations" two years before, Dr. David McBride now lives on New York's Lower East Side with his wife Cassandra and his demented father, Hal McBride. Hal McBride is now in the care of his son because he can no longer care for himself.

In the medical profession, David, a once-promising transplant surgeon, has been reduced to a lab technician. And Cassandra maintains her job as a scrub nurse. They make do, but making do isn't good enough for either one of them, especially not for the 28-year-old Cassandra, as she seems to be aging at a rapid pace due to the constant stress in their everyday lives. Her biggest fears: poverty and not having a child. Cassandra McBride loves her husband in the natural, but her spirit is under assault from the woes of self-hatred.
As usual, the spiritual attacks come on subtly at first, but then they start to build and build until they eventually take their toll on the minds of their human prey: in Cassandra McBride's case, the anger and fear and self-pity and

bitterness have pushed her to the brink so much so that she hates not only herself but also her marriage, her husband, and her pathetic, invalid of a father-in-law.

For now, though, she's functioning.

Of course, the spiritual enemy of all Mankind is not satisfied with leaving even one human being alone. No, he must first be allowed to enter into a person's house, that he may wage war and work his mass destruction on every individual involved, even from the head of the household on down to the very least in it. Indeed, this is the modus operandi of Mankind's sole enemy.

ALL THESE THINGS I WILL GIVE YOU...

Desperation will drive a man to desperate measures. It will make a man do things he would not have ever thought himself capable of: and now, at a convenient time, the spiritual enemy—hidden beneath the guise of desperation—has come to tempt the man named David McBride.

It's been two years since the blacklisting of David McBride from the branch of transplant surgery. And since that time, he has received one rejection letter after another - denying him a shot at redemption until now.
After reading that heart-breaking rejection letter from the University of North Dakota School of Medicine, Department of Surgery - not so long ago - David opens his mailbox on one fateful day to find hope. With the delivery of one piece of mail, the sun has risen to rebuke the gray, dreary gloom.

The sparkling letter, sent from the State University of New York, Downstate Medical Center, Department of Surgery, offers David a position in its general surgery program on one condition: David must be willing to repeat his fourth year of residency.
Written by Juan Carlos Valenzuela, Chairman of the Department of Surgery at SUNY, the words are like beautiful music to David's ears, and he can't stop his hands from shaking. Yes, he would do it! Anything to get his life back. And Cassandra? Oh, hell, she is going to flip!

The letter is uplifting. And it's all innocent enough until a most despised foe from David's past returns to toss a monkey wrench in any plans David may have—should he receive a second chance.
That despised foe? Dr. Andrew Turnbull - the man responsible for David's fall from grace in the first place.

Mr. White and Turnbull are now in panic mode after the death of Michael Smith. The two evildoers desire to remain co-conspirators in the illegal trade of kidney harvesting. But they can by no means proceed without a gifted surgeon to assist them in their treacherous violation of humanity.
For this reason, Dr. Andrew Turnbull recommends Dr. David McBride. And Mr. White, a man who's desperate to preserve the privileged life of one of his loved ones, is forced to make David McBride an offer that he will by no means be at liberty to refuse.
Now frightened into subjection and enticed by a large sum of money, not to mention a threat made that could destroy his work in medicine permanently, David McBride—trapped between a rock and a hard place—grudgingly agrees to do the devil's bidding. But it

would soon prove to be the worst decision he has ever made.

For what shall a man give in exchange for his eternal soul?

WHEN IT RAINS IT POURS.

The chain reaction of events that occur throughout this dialogue will leave the reader appalled and utterly disgusted. For whithersoever greed, false idolatry, lies, hopelessness, and betrayal assemble themselves to rendezvous, trust that despair and mayhem will be obliged to join them there.

THEY PLAYED THEIR PARTS WELL.

Included in the gifted cast of characters on these pages are the following:

- Sam Keating is a vicious ex-con and Andrew Turnbull's right-hand man at NuLife Corporation.

- Dr. Cynthia Evans is a fastidious health nut and specialized scientist at NuLife Corporation.

- Dr. Jeffrey Abercrombie is an unhygienic and morbidly obese—but brilliant—biochemist at NuLife Corporation.

- Dr. Steinberg is a resident of the psych service and a gatherer of unwilling donors.

- Detective Kate D'Angelo is the lead detective on the kidney harvesting case.

- Tyronne Pradeaux is an inner-city thug who has been in the debt of David McBride ever since David saved his life in the trauma ward from six gunshot wounds to his torso.

- Wendy is the homecare nurse commissioned to care for Hal McBride in the absence of David and Cassandra.

SUMMING UP AN IMPRESSIVE COMPOSITION.

The Organ Takers is a splendid work of fiction representative of a vivid imagination, a deft hand, and a considerable amount of medical research by its author. The narrative was by far one of the best books that I'd read in 2015. And I would eagerly recommend it to every fan of the medical thriller genre. Yes, even eagerly.

Congratulations on a phenomenal release, Richard Van Anderson. While I hated for Book 1 to end, it is with great enthusiasm that I look forward to completing the balance of your genuinely entertaining series.

Five body-snatching stars.

Cat Ellington's review of Finders Keepers by Sean Costello

My rating: 5 of 5 stars

Date read: May, 2015

Unputdownable
/ˌənˌpo͝otdounəbəl/

adjective INFORMAL
(of a book) so engrossing that one cannot stop reading it.

A PERFECT EXAMPLE.

Sean Costello's Finders Keepers is one such novel beyond a shadow of a doubt.
My introduction to the fictional works of said author, this singular plot—set in Costello's respective nativity of Canada—orbits around the lives of its trio of top-billed personae, including Keith Whipple, Kate Whipple, and Steve Segar.

THE BIG WIN.

There is absolutely no one more on the easy-going side than beloved widower and retiree, Keith Whipple. And as this fascinating tale begins to unfold, our leading man is entering Rudy's Quick-Mart, a popular convenience store in his area, to purchase the usual: coffee, black and nasty.

As is always the case, Rudy, the store's friendly owner, greets Keith with bright eyes and a warm smile. And the two men make conversation about this, that, and the other. Theirs is a long history of friendship, fifteen years strong. And there can be no better bonding, save for the one that Keith Whipple shares with his only child, an adult daughter named Kate. Kate Whipple - just as darling as her doting dad -is a movie buff and talented writer who dreams of one day becoming a Hollywood screenwriter.

Hey, a girl can have her dream, even if that dream never makes itself manifest in reality. A girl can dream. And Katie is determined to hold on tight to her big dream - even if at times doubtful that it will ever come true.
Faith is a good thing. And what Katie doesn't know is that her loving dad is about to become the most remarkable answer to her big dream. Heck, Keith Whipple doesn't even know what beauty lies ahead for him and his baby girl, Kate. Because he only bought a lottery ticket at Rudy's Quick-Mart on a whim. Hey, why not? Right? Because you never know. Right?

Now standing in Rudy's Quick-Mart checking his numbers at the lottery display, Keith Whipple is about to transform from an everyday guy into a multimillionaire—within seconds. Ten million big ones! Just like that! Keith and Kate Whipple will never, ever, have to struggle for anything again. Never again.
Dreams. They do come true. And Christmas is going to be extra special this year.

THE ACCIDENT.

Christmas day is fast approaching. And now that the Whipples are brand-spanking-new millionaires, er, multimillionaires, they can make the trek from their humble abode in Sudbury to Toronto, where Keith has two brothers, one sister, and a bunch of nieces and nephews. Oh, what a joyous time Christmas is going to be this year! There is plenty of money for all of them now. And they will spend it! They will eat. They will take vacations. They will buy summer homes. Everything! The sky's the limit!

Oh, the plans of Man.
Indeed, Man makes plans, but Man knows not the future.

JUST HOW SMALL ARE YOU?

Keith rents a limo—driven by a fellow named Bernie—to transport him home from Rudy's Quick-Mart. He soon picks up Kate, and they both head to the mall to do a little Christmas shopping en route to fabulous Toronto. And full of glee, as is natural for anyone who has just won a ten million dollar lottery purse, Keith Whipple is tempted to run his mouth off to Bernie about his good fortune, distracting the driver's eyes from the road all too often. A wicked snow storm is looming. And the trio of limousine occupants is on course to drive right into it. Keith and Bernie—excited about the lottery win—are still chatting off when the oil tanker makes its way around the snowy bend. Kate is the first one to see it. And terror is the last emotion that will throw a mean punch to stun the minds of all three before the two vehicles collide and the limo goes airborne on impact – finally coming to land in an icy ditch along the long stretch of road.

Here is where one Marty Small makes his godless, albeit show-stopping, entrance.

C'MON MAN, HAVE A HEART.

Rather than assisting the injured, you know, helping out his fellow man during the holiday season, Marty the Grinch relieves an unconscious Keith Whipple of his overcoat and wallet. He then lies to a semi-conscious Kate by telling her that he will contact the highway patrol and the paramedics. After that, he grabs the loot of already wrapped Christmas gifts and then gets back into his old beat-up car and hauls ass outta there.

But what the thieving, crooked, and lying drug addict—who is Marty Small—has yet to discern is that he is now the new holder of a ten million dollar-winning lottery ticket. Indeed, that amount of money could (and would) buy Earlene the Cocaine Queen a hundred more whorish lifetimes.

DESTRUCTION AND MISERY ARE IN THEIR WAYS.

For everyone evil, even depraved and perverse, there is always another one much worse.
No one knows this better than Detective Sergeant Alister "Al" Raybould, this narrative's self-hating and frightfully demonic antagonist.

Save for his male erectile organ—which is mightily blessed, to say the least—Detective Sergeant Al Raybould is the sort of accursed soul that the pit of Sheol cannot feast itself upon fast enough.

Detective Sergeant Al Raybould, a dirty cop on the take, has snuffed out any number of lives before, and he will continue to do so—so long as don Constantine "Connie" Corsino keeps an oppressive thumb on his iniquitous head. For as Detective Sergeant Al Raybould exists to be an individual thorn in the flesh of many, so, too, does don Constantine Corsino exist to be a thorn in his.

LOVE AT FIRST SIGHT.

Regardless of the incoming storm, Sergeant Mitch Buchanan of the Ontario Provincial Police Patrol is on duty. And so is his young rookie partner, Constable Steve Segar. The two men should have been done with their shift already, but duty calls - especially in such a climatical mess as the rapidly building snowstorm.
After the horrible accident they just left only moments before, Steve only wants the stressful workday to be over. But no can do. The day drags on and on.

Now dispatched to a tanker accident along their route, Sergeant Buchanan and Constable Segar eventually come upon the wrecked limousine and quickly begin to make their assessments, checking out the conditions of the three occupants.
For Constable Steve Segar, this one isn't unlike any other accident he has had the misfortune of surveying until he sees her beautiful face. The bloodied but lovely face of a semi-conscious Kate Whipple. She can barely speak, but she's audible enough, asking about the well-being of her father. The accident scene is gruesome, yes, but it doesn't repel Cupid. The mythical son of Mars and Venus flies in quickly - that he may strike the heart of Constable Steve

Segar with his arrow of love bearing the name of one Kate Whipple.

His lovestruck swooning aside, the handsome Constable Segar can by no means foresee the hazardous danger zone up ahead, hiding right around the corner of the sharp turn both he and Kate Whipple are about to make.

THOSE WHO DESIRE TO BE RICH ... FALL INTO A SNARE.

It's not long before Marty Small realizes that he has a winning lottery ticket. And it's all thanks to the shifty media and some no-name convenience store clerk. The time has come for Marty to be able to have the coke-snorting whore, Earlene, a skanky lap dancer at *Fantasia*. She'll have no other choice but to spend her wretched life with him now—whether she likes it or not.
Because he, Marty Small, of all people, is finally somebody. Yes, he is the one on top now! And no one can stop him. No, not even one.

Or so he thinks.

If truth be told, there is one, no, four: Al Raybould, a man with a wave of anger as fierce as that of a roaring lion; Tarek Yaghi, the Middle-Eastern owner of *Yaghi's Market*; Claudette Yaghi, the disgustingly obese and hateful White-Canadian wife of Tarek Yaghi; and Kate Whipple, a woman who never forgets a face—especially not that of the one belonging to Marty Small.

- Marty Small. He will keep that winning lottery ticket, even if it means that he must kill to do so.

- Al Raybould. He will steal that winning lottery ticket, even if it means that he must kill to do so.

- Tarek Yaghi. He needs that winning lottery ticket to finally be free of the morbidly obese, infamously jealous, and excessively needy Claudette.

- Claudette Yaghi. She will get that winning lottery ticket, even if it means that she must wobble her disgusting bulk into the unrelenting embrace of death to do so.

- Kate Whipple. She will get that winning lottery ticket back, even if it means that she must disembowel the guts of Hell to do so.

FINDERS KEEPERS. A FICTIONAL SENSATION.

Sean Costello is brilliant! *Finders Keepers*, perhaps one of the greatest works of fiction enjoyed by my reader in the new age of digitalization, sparkles like a fine cut gem in its respective class of crime thrillers. With a plot drenched in a downpour of nail-biting suspense, the tale is a wild goose chase of page-turning excitement, heart-pounding thrills, merciless activities, and mind-boggling sequences. In itself, the dialogue is remarkably written and intertwined with a consummate cast of passive/aggressive players, including the following:

- Thomas Swain, a heroin addict, sassy sissy, and timid mouse to Al Raybould's wildcat

- Nelson Flexner, a wealthy attorney who has become the stalked prey of Al Raybould

- Abigail Flexner, the wife of Nelson Flexner and a serpentine witch

- Rodney Hicks, the Internal Affairs detective investigating his former partner-turned-archenemy, Al Raybould

- Bryan Mayer, an Internal Affairs detective; and a new partner to Rodney Hicks

- Stan Howson, the top cop in Internal Affairs

- Liz Segar, a badass head detective in the OPP precinct and the adored mother of Steve Segar

- Miss Aretha, the receptionist in Sexual Assault at Metro headquarters and godmother to Steve Segar

- Gord Brown, an operative in lottery fraud investigations and the man assigned to solve the mystery of the stolen ten million dollar ticket

- Morris "Mo" Brooks, Kate's former boss at Panther Courier and an undisputed asshole

- Marilyn, the chubby, buxom, and bleach-blonde mistress of Tarek Yaghi

- Detective Jack Cullen, the tie that binds together the likes of Marty Small, Tarek Yaghi, and Claudette Yaghi

A LARGE SUM OF PRAISE.

Although it employs a considerable ensemble, *Finders Keepers* is a magnificent read that I would highly recommend to any fan of gritty crime thrillers - as it is a well-balanced tale genuine to its grade from start to finish. And because of it, I became a loyal fan of its gifted authorship. Excellent writing. Kudos, Mr. Costello!

Five filthy rich—but deadly—stars.

Cat Ellington's review of Status 3 by Jordan Belcher

My rating: 5 out of 5 stars

Date read: May, 2015

THE SPIRIT WITHIN.

Three days may seem like a short period, but many things can happen over 72 hours, e.g., bachelorette parties, wedding ceremonies, wedding receptions, and even cold-blooded murders.

On the pages of this, the final installment in Jordan Belcher's *Status* trilogy, we get pulled through yet another (mind-boggling) vortex coated with madness, obsession, fear, envy, jealousy, covetousness, low self-esteem, idolatry, self-hatred, hatred, anger, rage, malice, fear, anxiety, paranoia, revenge, misery, and self-destruction. And the ones spinning around in it are the same ones whose souls are lost there in the dens of sin.

Indeed, on these quick-witted pages of (insatiable) suspense, creative magnificence knows no bounds. And Jordan Belcher continues to prove his genius in the inimitable classification of Urban Fiction.

Dear reader? Shall we?

THE DEVIL GETS BUSY.

Rita Wilson, known by her Site username as *RealSpit*, is feeling pretty good today. At present, Rita is buying expensive wedding gifts for Rodrick Brown and his wife-to-be, Tyesha Fenty. The day is gorgeous, and Rita could not be happier for her beautiful Site friends. Rodrick and Tyesha are finally going to do it; they are finally going to jump that ol' broom! After all these years. Who in the world would have thought it possible? Rodrick Brown, of all men, getting married?

Yes, it's enough to make one chuckle, but Rita doesn't. She wants to keep her focus sharp and get all of these lovely registry gifts loaded into her Volvo XC90 parked outside.

But it isn't until after the packages are tucked safely inside of her vehicle that Rita notices it. One of her tires is flat. But the tire in question hasn't deflated (on its own) from a loss of air. No, this tire was deliberately cut. Shocked, Rita can't possibly imagine who could've done such a thing. But before she can dial the number for roadside assistance, a familiar face appears. Speaking in a voice familiar to Rita, the person offers to help.

Sure, the gesture of kindness appears friendly enough. But smiling faces, smiling faces, sometimes, they don't tell the truth. And before long, all notorious hell breaks loose.

GOIN' TO THE CHAPEL AND WE'RE GONNA GET MARRIED.

Our leading lady, the ever stalked and coveted Tyesha Fenty, cannot believe this is happening. In just three days, she's going to be Mrs. Rodrick Brown!

Tyesha Brown. Hey, that has a nice little ring to it. And speaking of things like rings, her friends are going to be amazed to see the dazzling sparkler gracing the third finger of her left hand, although *it's* not so little. Tyesha Fenty's engagement ring is nothing short of humongous. The gem is gorgeous. And it was slipped on her finger by none other than Rodrick Brown, otherwise known by his Site name as *"Rodrick Al-Bashir."*

On this joyful day, both Tyesha and Kylie are at the Kansas City International Airport with Rodrick as he prepares to board a flight to Ouro Preto, Brazil. The real purpose of the trip is for business, but, of course, Rodrick Brown - braggadocious as they come - felt compelled to boast about it in a status update. And his reason for doing this? To give his "friends"—and every other nigga having eyes with which to read—the impression that the journey is more for the point of pleasure. But could it be? Indeed, Rodrick Brown is still at it, thinking like a single and liberated bachelor—despite it being only 72 hours before his wedding day.

IT'S A BACHELORETTE PARTY, IT'S GONNA LAST ALL NIGHT LONG.

Just because she quit social media altogether doesn't mean that Tyesha Fenty, otherwise known by her Site username "*Tyesha816*," has stopped socializing with her Site clique in the real world. Never that. Darlene "*AtlantaBaby*" Rooney, an event planner to die for, is gearing up to throw Tyesha one of the most lavish—and kinky—bachelorette parties ever. And the gang's all here, including the vigilant Christina "*MsFineGirl*" Irving, a chosen bridesmaid.

These all party, the future bride and her Site girls, drinking in the chiseled anatomy of each male dancer and making merry with catered meals and premium liquor.
But there, lurking in the corner and drinking in the wildness of their revelry and their effortless display of self-confidence is one who secretly hates the feeling of being a so-called nobody and an unimportant commoner trying desperately to fit in with the "beautiful people." For this one is the same who is full of anger, bitterness, and self-hatred. This one is the same who is a murderer and a hater - pretending to be a *friend*.

SURPRISE, BITCH!

Tyesha Fenty is a (very) popular—and undeniably attractive—woman. And many strive to be in her company, in her social circle, and part of her private life. There are also quite a few others, particularly women, who envy and covet her. And who secretly wish they could be her.

Such women hate not only themselves as women but also other women, especially those who foster self-love. Such women are those whose own lives stew in failures and miseries and hopelessness and faithlessness. Such women compare their own lives to that of other women—only to realize their persistent shortcomings. Such women are those who need to believe that they've more power in their vaginal cavities than any other woman—only to be proven wrong time and again. Such women are those who are so full of pride and machismo - that they repeatedly repel men.

Women. They can sometimes be their own worst enemy. And the masterfully selected ensemble of women who appear on these superb and fast-paced pages of urban suspense are among some of those who fall into the above categories: for from within an envious woman scorned, there breaks forth a ferocious rage.
And on these pages, Tyesha Fenty is too entangled in her marital squabbles to see the bared fangs and claws coming.

SOCIAL MEDIA. A DISTORTION OF REALITY.

The invention of social media was to allow its users to create and share content. And to participate in social networking. That had been the "original plan" of those brilliant application and website developers who have established their tech houses on the bedrock of Silicon Valley. Unfortunately, though, there are (many) troubled individuals out there using the systems for anything other than their first intention. Case in point: lies and deception.

So many people would like for others—particularly strangers—to believe their delusions and their false presentations featured on social media platforms – the same from which their reality contrasts sharply. It's so easy pretending to be something (or someone) else that one is not, all to try to impress others - as well as to feel good about oneself. Some will even profess to be your "*friend*" today … and murder you in cold blood tomorrow.

Trust, dear reader, that the co-starring cast members who render literary-award-worthy performances on the maliciously cunning pages of this final installment are no exception.
They are as follows:

- Kylie Brown, precious daughter to Tyesha Fenty and Rodrick Brown

- Dylan Irving, Christina Irving's elder brother

- Detective Rosan, our lead gumshoe investigating the stalking case of Tyesha Fenty

- Randy Moore, a social media troll and possible stalker

- Ruth Jameson, Tyesha's former boss at the Kansas City DMV - and a woman with an ax to grind

- Darlene Rooney, Kansas City resident by way of Atlanta and top-notch event planner

- Skooly, Rodrick's number one man on the streets

- Klint, Skooly's brother, and a midwest hood

- Quita Wheeler, a so-called Site friend - and an exposed coveter of Rodrick Brown

- Wendy Hartley, a Site resident, a lover of revelry, and a girl you'll love to taste

- Joanne Dunley, a needy dishrag and hapless man-pleaser to Tyesha

- Stuart Bradshaw, boyfriend to Joanne Dunley and security guard at the Kansas City DMV

- Landon Roby, Tyesha's beloved younger brother - and self-proclaimed ladykiller

- Kayla and Kendal Roby, Landon Roby's beautiful daughters

- Maxine Brown, Rodrick's proud mama

- Dava Babcock, a secondary baby momma to Rodrick Brown, Jr., and a woman with an ax to grind

THEY GOT SKILLS.

This incredible cast, complemented by an entire bastion of key bit players and standout extras who are always eager to meddle, instigate, and signify, gleefully uphold the legend that is the Black/urban drama.

Status 3, the final installment in the must-read *Status* trilogy, is exceptional, even slightly exalted above the standard of literary greatness. And in response to it, I am inclined to (once again) tip my cloché to its mightily blessed authorship.

Five anything-but-blissful stars.

Chapter 5
In Flourishing Mode

Cat Ellington's review of Every Breath You Take by Bianca Sloane

My rating: 5 out of 5 stars

Date read: March, 2015

EVERY STEP YOU TAKE, I'LL BE WATCHING YOU.

In this oppressively apprehensive tale about a love lost, love found, and one man's maniacal obsession, we come to make the acquaintance of its 28-year-old leading lady Natalie Scott, a beautiful public relations manager for a major hotel chain in Chicago. Like many of us, Natalie Scott has a past – a not so happy past that she would sooner cut off her ears than listen to anyone recant.

It's been ten long years since she last saw him. But the memories still haunt her to this very day, tormenting her spirit and vying to ruin any chance that she may have at securing peace in her life. The old fears? They refuse to die. And it troubles them to see her live. These old trepidations toil long and hard in their efforts to attack her mind, especially when she's alone. And it has gotten to a point where Natalie doesn't know who she can trust anymore – outside of her tightly united circle of besties, that is.

Jesus, what would she do without Christine, Brandy, and Dina? Her three best friends in the world. They are her life, the only people whom she can trust. And without them, she would be lost.

He made her life this way. He ruined her sensibilities, her free-spirited nature, her trust in men, her life.

Natalie is a woman so young, so beautiful, so successful, and so alone. Natalie is a woman so haunted, so frightened, so confused, and so stalked: for he's come back to claim her as his own - for good.

A KNIGHT IN SHINING ARMOR.

From the moment he glimpsed her across the crowded room, financial analyst Jason Hudson just knew he had to have her. She was so tall and so gorgeous that he couldn't help but be nervous as he approached her to strike up a well-meaning, albeit clumsy, conversation. Her name is Natalie. And she's polite but standoffish. She probably thinks he's a jerk for being so nervous. But she's a little bit nervous too. He finds her striking, and she thinks he's cute. He offers her his business card, and she accepts it, although hesitantly. She agrees to call him, and they part ways. But Natalie can feel him watching her back. Natalie Scott is scared and wary; she's been too damaged by her past. Her past? It won't leave her be. The memories fail to escape her. And this Jason guy? He might be another crazed maniac - like *him*. No, she won't call him. She mustn't. Natalie must protect herself lest anyone else should try to hurt her again.

But what the extraordinarily paranoid Natalie Scott fails to understand, at the moment, is that the terribly handsome—albeit somewhat awkward—Jason Hudson is about to become the best thing that has ever happened to her.

(AFRICAN) AMERICAN PSYCHO.

After years of being institutionalized for the brutal murder of Natalie's first love, the result of his intense jealousy and deranged obsession, Joey Green is finally being released. He has managed to convince his doctors of his stabilized mental health, and they, in turn, have decided that Joey is well enough to be reinserted into society.
Joey Green. He's played every one of his deceptive cards well. And he's won against them. He's won against them all! And once he's free, once he's out of this sadistic madhouse, he and his Nat will finally be reunited. *Natalie.* She's his and only his. Forever meant to be. He and Natalie.
Joey and Natalie. Hey, that rhymes.

Natalie. He's dreamt about her for years. His Natalie. His beautiful Natalie. His and absolutely no one else's—especially not that of another man! But only his. His. HIS!

How long will it take to get to Chicago?

RELIVING THE NIGHTMARE.

Natalie can dream again. There *is* such a thing as a second wind. And Jason Hudson—*her* Jason Hudson—has helped her to realize this. Oh, how happy she is once again. Oh, how much fun she and Jason have together. The orphaned (and only) daughter of a superstar quarterback and a most stunning head cheerleader, Natalie can finally own it again on her terms - and the right arm of Jason.

But Joey Green? The newly free Joey Green? Well, he has other plans. He has built the perfect home—far away—for just the two of them, both himself and Natalie. A lovely dream home where they can both live happily ever after. And where no one will ever find them.
A lovely dream home far away from that cold, dirty, and noisy Chicago.

It is only he, Joey, who can make Natalie so truly happy. He's been watching her, watching her every move. And he's patient, even like a fierce predator stalking its unsuspecting prey. He's patient. He can handle the skank besties—that damn Latina Christine, that blonde bombshell Brandy, and that other uppity bitch, Dina. Yeah, he can keep them at bay. But what about that tall and built pretty boy? The one with whom his Nat has become so damn smitten? Well, he'll have to handle him, too—like he did the other one.

Natalie, honey? Heeere's Joey!

THE PERFECT SCRIPT BEGETS THE PERFECT CAST.

A story narrated in multiple-character viewpoints (from Natalie Scott to Joey Green), the remarkable vision of Bianca Sloane comes alive on the masterful pages of this incredible literary presentation.
Sloane weaves a tale of nail-biting suspense and mind-altering madness unlike no other with *Every Breath You Take*. And I can't imagine that any reader will conclude it unfazed.

Doing their creator tremendous justice on the pages of this commendable script is one of the most gifted supporting ensembles with whom my reader has ever become familiar in the exciting world of fictional literature, including:

- Zach and Cheryl Scott, the bitter, envious, malicious, and abusive uncle and aunt in whose joint care an orphaned Natalie had been after the untimely deaths of her famous parents and her affectionate grandparents

- Dr. Wexler, the German psychiatrist who is assigned to monitor Joey Green during his mental institution sentence

- Brian, an all-around great guy - and Christine's fun-loving soulmate and fiancé

- Kevin, Chuck, Pete, and Ollie, a quartet of love and devotion, and Jason's trusted cronies since childhood

- Ty, a crook, a snake, and a willing accomplice in the wicked game of Joey Green

- Dennis Jones, a college track star, an intellectual, Natalie's first love, and a marked man

Complementing this cast is a small troupe of players who co-star as Jason's family – the same made up of his parents, grandparents, a few siblings, and a bunch of nieces and nephews.
A beautiful and close-knit clan, the Hudsons are the *"Callaghans"* to Natalie's *"Lucy Eleanor Moderatz."*
For you readers born after 1995, the characters (the "Callaghans" and "Lucy Eleanor Moderatz") are references to the unforgettable stars of the Jon Turteltaub-directed rom-com, *While You Were Sleeping*.

I CAN'T SAY ENOUGH GOOD THINGS.

Bianca Sloane is nothing short of perfection in the unmatched craft of creative writing. And it's safe to say that before long, there will be myriads of suspense enthusiasts willing to agree.

It takes a lot for me to fall in love with a writer after I read their work. But with Bianca Sloane and her breakout thriller, *Killing Me Softly*, that is what occurred. I fell in love with her literary vision. And once again, she has wowed my reader into a muted state of jaw-dropping speechlessness.
Indeed, Bianca Sloane is an exceptional storyteller. And within me is a fan that both she and her remarkable literature will forever have.

Every Breath You Take is a masterpiece in its class and a must-read, indeed.

Five blood-weeping stars.

Cat Ellington's review of Sweet Little Lies by Bianca Sloane

My rating: 5 out of 5 stars

Date read: April, 2015

YOU CAN'T DISGUISE, NO YOU CAN'T DISGUISE.

Kelly Ross is a woman who has it all: breathtaking beauty, international fame, a vast fortune, a lucrative cosmetics business, a dazzling high rise residence along the legendary lakefront of Chicago's Gold Coast, another ritzy apartment in New York, another ritzy apartment in London, and a handsome, sexy, and powerful husband in Mark Monroe.

Unfortunately, one cannot say the same for her level of self-esteem - which is quite bottomless.

When considering the outward appearance, no one would ever believe that a woman like Kelly Ross—the great supermodel—could be so insecure and feel threatened by another woman. But what the *flesh* fails to reveal, the *spirit* doesn't – that the true nature of people should be exposed openly and judged accordingly.

WHO'S BEEN SLEEPING IN MY BED?

Chicago is always gorgeous during the Spring season, what with her fabulous parks lined with an array of flowering trees, and her stunning gardens in perfect bloom, and her vast stretch of lakeshore laid out by an endless reservoir of vivid, sparkling azure.

Indeed, she is a most prepossessing town, even one pretty as a picture. And as the curtains of this thriller get pulled back to let the springtime sunshine in, we make the acquaintance of our leading lady, Ms. Kelly Ross-Monroe, who, incidentally, has just wrapped up a girls' shopping date with her best friend, the best-selling author Sheila Stevens. Kelly is on her way home – back to the 53rd-floor condo that she shares with her prosperous husband Mark Monroe, a thirty-three-year-old partner at Bell, Banks, and Crawford, one of the most highly-esteemed law firms in Chicago.

Slathered with the sensual scent of contentment, Kelly Ross makes it her job to shun the lowliness of piety. Kelly Ross—a proud woman was there ever one—is a creature of habit, preferring to rely solely upon her status in society and ever-stroked ego. But the thing that got Kelly Ross way up there is the same thing that will seek to snatch her down.

At present, Ms. Ross, Ms. Monroe, whichever you prefer, is in her luxurious bedroom admiring its décor and entertaining warm and loving thoughts about her good-looking and successful husband. Her sensational life is perfect. And so is her sensationalized marriage, even the same that warranted a ton of articles in some of the most revered gossip columns and celebrity tabloids read by the common man.

Mark's and her marriage bed? It is perfect. The luxurious carpeting upon which her dainty feet do their walking? It is

perfect. The fabulous view from their floor to ceiling windows? It is perfect.
Hell, every little thing about them is perfect, perfect, PERFECT!

At least that has been the belief of Kelly Ross until now.

Before it fell out of a pile of dirty sheets that she'd picked up off the floor to have washed, everything was perfect. Before it landed, lazily, on her dainty foot—with its professional pedicure—everything was perfect. Before she ever saw it, everything was perfect.
It is a condom. A *used* condom.

SEEING RED. BLOOD RED.

As if on cue, the demonic entities of pride, arrogance, vanity, and fear uncoil themselves, like venomous Cobras, and slither into the mind of Kelly Ross. They wage a ruthless war on her body, her spirit, and her soul by way of a poisonous onslaught of all manner of troubling speculation.
The enraged demonic thoughts—instigated by ego—hiss, and whisper, into the mind of the human: *How dare that son of a bitch?! You're a goddamn supermodel! Men don't cheat on no goddamn supermodels! People mistake you for Vanessa Williams! Look at you! Look at how tall and lithe and stunning you are! Look at your smooth skin, Champagne in hue! How could he even look at another woman?!*

The demons of pride, ego, arrogance, and vanity are hard at work, tempting and egging on - until they finally hit pay dirt.

IT'S ALL IN THE MIND.

The human mind. It is truly a terrible thing to waste, especially on spiritual warfare. But by the time Mark Monroe returns home from the office, Kelly Ross, a spiritually ignorant woman untrained to know the power of a divine rebuke, has already fallen prey to the evil thoughts of anger and rage—brought on, of course, by her shattered ego.

Indeed, by the time Mark Monroe enters their (immaculate) abode, the fire raging inside of Kelly Ross is already kindled.

I AM AN INNOCENT MAN.

Mark Monroe—a multi-millionaire specialized in sports and media law—has not committed what is sinful against his flesh. Neither has he committed any infidelity behind the back of his equally celebrated wife. But regardless of his constant pleading, an insecure Kelly Ross, still under assault in her worldly mind, is adamant in her utter refusal to believe him. Mark, confused and looking for a way to explain the culprit condom to his enraged wife, can barely get a word in as Kelly Ross has already made it up in her mind that he's a cheating husband worthy of her psychotic scorn.
Indeed, Kelly Ross—now slightly drunk with wine—is nothing if not frantically pissed.

Mark desperately pleads in his defense, but Kelly cuts him—figuratively—with one acidic word after another. Mark continues to plead, but Kelly stabs him—literally—with a butcher knife from their expensive cutlery set.

And time stands still.

HOW THE WAR WAS WAGED. HOW SHE LOST THE BATTLE.

Kelly Ross immediately returns to her senses—only to realize that the spiritual war waged on her mind has been (miserably) lost.

- Pride begot ego
- Ego begot arrogance
- Arrogance begot vanity
- Vanity begot self-hatred
- Self-hatred begot low self-esteem
- Low self-esteem begot self-pity
- Self-pity begot doubt
- Doubt begot anxiety
- Anxiety begot paranoia
- Paranoia begot fear
- Fear begot hatred
- Hatred begot anger
- Anger begot rage
- Rage begot revenge
- And revenge began with a murderous spirit

This had been the spiritual war waged on the carnal mind of Kelly Ross. And she lost.

IT'S NOT OVER 'TIL IT'S OVER.

For good measure, the conjoined spirits of fear, anxiety, and paranoia shoot another fiery arrow at the mind of the human puppet with just one derisive word: *Run!*

THE SUSPECTED MISTRESS.

The haughty bitch that is Kelly Ross-Monroe's ego will not leave her be. It speaks to her mind, saying, *What woman on Earth had that much game, what to lure Mark away from you? Who the hell is she? Could it be Portia, his devoted assistant and a major coveter of his loins? Could she be the outstanding Lindsay Wayne? The tall, dark-skinned, and awesomely lovely Lindsay Wayne? Lindsay Wayne. Mark's former law office colleague, Lincoln Park princess, nippy wife to Julian, and perhaps one of only a few women who could give you a run for your massive pile of fame and money. Could it be her? Who is the bitch?*

When Mark's ringing—but unanswered—phone receives a strange voicemail message, Kelly startles from her enemy-centered reverie and gets her answer when she rushes to retrieve it. But rather than hearing the syrupy voice of a rich, famous, worldly, sophisticated, and educated woman like herself, the ear of (the great) Kelly Ross is greeted with the loud, uneducated, sloppy, and detestable speech of a Black-American hood rat – straight outta the segregated confines of a poverty-stricken, inner-city ghetto.

"Call me, Boo."

The woman's words are like decorated press-on nails maliciously dragging themselves on the dry chalkboard that is Ms. Ross.

INTRODUCING GENEVA MONROE.

Geneva Monroe. A wicked and triflin' woman who will rise like bile reflux in the esophagus - to first burn the throats of Chicago's finest, then drop kick the sidity-and-pretty ass of Kelly Ross into the middle of next week, before snatching it back to dropkick all over again.

THE PERILS OF LEADING A DOUBLE LIFE.

Who is Mark Monroe? And what dark secrets has he been hiding from the one and only Kelly Ross all of these years? His antagonized past? Why has it come back with a double-edged sword to slay his fabulously happy present?

Who the hell is Geneva?
And who the hell is Mark Monroe, Jr.?

HOW TO BECOME A GREAT BYWORD.

It is written:

"Surely, You set them in slippery places; You cast them down to destruction.

Oh, how they are
brought to desolation, as
in a moment! They are utterly
consumed with terrors."
—Psalms 73:18-19

A PANDORA'S BOX OF SUPERLATIVE DRAMA, MYSTERY, AND SUSPENSE.

In this fictional ballroom embellished with habitual lies, sneaky deception, closely-guarded secrets, scorching hatred, murderous jealousy, conniving greed, covetous idolatry, and softly-lit materialism, the proud and stiff-necked come together to dance a perfidious waltz. And before long, they each commence twirling one another right over a jagged edge of man-eating regret and comprehensive destruction.

Yoked together with them in the dens of ruination are none other than the fascinating group of supporting players who are nothing short of what we have come to expect in the awe-inspiring literature of Ms. Bianca Sloane:

- Sheila Stevens, a famous crime novelist and the best friend of Kelly Ross

- Gary Stevens, husband to Sheila and the skirt to her pants

- Sam Gordon, the nationally famous criminal defense attorney, hired by Kelly Ross to handle her complicated case

- Bill Hanson, the blond-haired, blue-eyed, and no-nonsense Chicago PD detective investigating the Ross-Monroe murder case

- Didi Martin, a Chicago PD detective and Bill Hanson's partner on the Ross-Monroe murder case

- Harry Ross and Candice Ross, the wealthy and bourgeois parents of Kelly Ross and two of Evanston's very own

- Stacy Ross, an interior designer in New York and the younger sister of Kelly Ross

- Harvey Jackson, an ulcerous and ragtag public defender assigned to Geneva Monroe

- Patric Pierre, an international movie star and former love interest of Kelly Ross

- Roy Monroe, a meager resident of Indiana and the younger brother of Mark Monroe

- Brad Banks, managing partner at Bell, Banks, and Crawford

- Tim Landry, Mark Monroe's brother from another mother and a man privy to his many dark and deeply harbored secrets

I EXTOL HER AUTHORSHIP.

From Chicago to New Orleans to New York and back, Old Scratch keeps himself busy with Sloane's unforgettable—and sometimes unforgivable—cast.

Once again, I must tip my cloché in honor of this author's formidable perfection—concerning both her admirable creative vision and her undeniable ability to mold a word in the structure of body text. Bianca Sloane is outstanding. And *Sweet Little Lies*, named for the 80s pop song made famous by the legendary Fleetwood Mac, is a literary masterpiece, period.
The strongly recommended narrative does its respective class of suspense incomparable justice. And of it, Sloane ought to be extensively proud.

Five 'til-death-do-us-part stars.

Cat Ellington's review of Murder on the Down Low by Pamela Samuels Young

My rating: 5 out of 5 stars

Date read: June, 2015

REVIEWER'S NOTE:

My dearest readers, I regret to inform you that my original review of *Murder on the Down Low* had also been among a bundle of examinations that I lost during a factory reset a few years back. As I mentioned earlier, I failed to back up those precious files in the proper outlets. Please keep in mind that I had been an Internet novice and still unlearned concerning many of its functions, ergo many mistakes were made.

However, I was able to retain a few of my notes. And it is with them that I have consulted to present my brief examination of this novel.

My patchwork analysis of *Murder on the Down Low* will now proceed.

A STYLE SO GRISHAMESQUE.

Pamela Samuels Young has a writing style similar to that of John Grisham: for as *The Firm* and *The Client* had wowed and intrigued my reader, so did the narrative currently under review.

MY FIRST GO-ROUND.

The gifted Pamela Samuels Young boldly commanded my newfound admiration (and adoration) with her fascinating legal thriller, *Murder on the Down Low*. And despite its being the third treatment in her respective Vernetta Henderson series, the dialogue was my first experience with Young's writing.

It had not been my intention to read the sequence out of order; it's only that *Murder on the Down Low* was a highly recommended complimentary copy courtesy of my then book club. Thank you, folks.

A legal thriller of intense suspense, *Murder on the Down Low*, set in a smoggy Los Angeles, has it all: racial tensions, hate crimes, murders, vindictiveness, jealousy, self-hatred, mayhem, and a fiercely perturbing plot adorned with a shattering twist – not to mention its shrewd leading lady, the sexy and no-nonsense legal beagle, Vernetta Henderson.

LOOKING FORWARD.

Murder on the Down Low is an exciting, action-packed thriller that I was loath to finish. The plot is superb, and the cast features memorable characters who are both lovable and scandalous alike.

Murder on the Down Low not only commanded my interest from beginning to end but also prompted me to immediately purchase *Every Reasonable Doubt (Vernetta Henderson Series Book 1)* and *In Firm Pursuit (Vernetta Henderson Series Book 2)*, in the wake of my concluding it. Great job, Pamela.

Know for a certainty that I will eventually come to view the other efforts as I continue to plow through my extensive reading queue. But in the meantime, my cloché must come off in honor of the fine job that Pamela Samuels Young has done with *Murder on the Down Low*.

Reading like a motion picture script, I could only think of one woman who would flawlessly portray Vernetta Henderson were *Murder on the Down Low* ever commissioned for a feature film adaptation: Vivica A. Fox. If truth be told, Vivica will kill it in her portrayal of Vernetta Henderson!

Indeed, she most certainly would.

Five culturally-envious stars.

Cat Ellington's review of Missing You (Every Breath You Take #1.5) by Bianca Sloane

My rating: 5 out of 5 stars

Date read: December, 2015

I spend my time thinking about you,
And it's almost driving me wild
—*Missing You* (1984)
Song by John Waite

THINKING BACK.

Whatever happened to Natalie Scott? In this unusually-good sequel to *Every Breath You Take*, the plot guides the reader through the entire sequence of events that occurred in the wake of Natalie's disappearance only weeks before. Narrated in the multiple viewpoints of a comatose Jason Hudson: whose thoughts speak to reminisce about Natalie's and his terrifying ordeal, and *Sweet Little Lies* star, Detective Bill Hanson, who returns to reprise his juicy role as a Chicago PD lead investigator—only this time in the mysterious abduction of Natalie Scott.

As the limping weeks evolve into crippled months, Natalie Scott is still missing and presumed dead. Investigators have no leads to her whereabouts. And the only two witnesses they have in the attack on her fiance, Jason Hudson, are his perceptible neighbors, Freeda Barnes and Adam Kerr.

Following the brutal—and bloody—attack on Jason Hudson by a complete stranger who broke into his luxurious condo, Jason himself was left for dead, and his beloved fiancée, Natalie, was kidnapped. Stolen away by a madman.

Jason thinks: *She screamed, his Natalie did. She screamed. He tried to save her, but he failed. The searing pain in his back prevented him from saving her. He fought, but the man overtook him and attacked. Who stabbed him in his back? Who was it that tried to murder him? Who took Natalie?*

Jason Hudson lies comatose in his hospital bed, trying to piece together this languishing puzzle of a mystery in his prolonged subconscious: *He's not supposed to be alive. He's supposed to be dead. The madman meant to kill him.*

WICKED GAME.

Joey Green never dreamed that he'd meet somebody like Natalie Scott.
Joey Green never dreamed that he'd lose somebody like Natalie Scott.
But he did.
He met her. He lost her. And he did what he had to do to "reclaim" her.

They're searching for her now, the whole lot of them. But they'll never find her because he has hidden her far away from them all. They're going nuts wondering where she is. He knows this because he has kept abreast of the news coverage. But the hell with them! All of them! He hates every one of them, especially those stuck up skanks

*Christine, Brandy, and Dina. But most of all, he hates that pretty boy bastard, Jason Hudson.
Did they believe that they could separate him from her? Yes, they did. And for that, he must teach them a lesson. Yeah, he will do just that. He will play with them for a little while. He will screw with their sidity minds.*

*Hey, a few prank calls never hurt anyone. Right?
He needs to make 'em squirm. Heh, spin 'em like tops. Why the hell is Jason Hudson still alive?
He thought he got rid of him. But he failed. Jason is still alive.
He's out of his coma, and he's alert. He's searching for Natalie. He's searching for his so-called "Scotty."*

The preceding represents the spirit of vengeful madness. And so does the following:

*He and Jason Hudson have unfinished business, sure, but he must continue to play his cards just right lest he loses the game.
And Joey Green cannot afford to lose the game. For he'd sooner butcher to death a hundred men before he allowed himself to lose the game – or "Nat."*

LOVE POWER.

Indeed, the power of love will make a man do some miraculous things. Well, that may not be the adage verbatim, but you get my point. Take Jason Hudson, for example. His love for Natalie Scott is so powerful that he dared to survive multiple stab wounds and battled his way from a comatose state back to the city of the living to save her from whomever it was that took her away. Encouraged by a beautiful support system consisting of his parents, his best friends, and his oldest sister, Jordan, Jason extracts himself from his hospital bed to go in search of his girl. *His Scotty.* But finding her won't be an effortless feat because his greatest unknown foe is already preparing his artillery of weaponry to finish up where he left off—in a most menacing approach.

The aim of the madman is simple: Natalie.
And if he can't have Natalie, no other man will be allowed to enjoy life with her either. Indeed, he'll see to that, even if he has to kill her dead to bring it to pass.

TICKLING HIS EARS.

Joey Green has taught his obsession, Natalie Scott, that you should always tell people what they *want* to hear rather than what they *need* to hear. And for her own sake, the courageous Natalie has elected to do just that.

Oh, yoo-hoo! Sheol? Open wide your mouth - to fill it with the table scraps of more evil.

FULL OF CHARACTER.

Quite a few cast members from *Every Breath You Take* have returned to reprise their unforgettable roles on these well-scribed pages, including Christine Diaz Garcia, Brandy Todd, Dina Preston, Good ol' Ollie, and the lovable Pete. And are complemented by an equally talented bunch of new castmates led by the following:

- Chicago Detective Bill Hanson (*Sweet Little Lies*) is the co-narrator of this gem

- Detective Slater, a twenty-six-year-old rookie - and a new partner to Bill Hanson

- Alex Preston, the attentive and nurturing, albeit long-suffering, husband of the diva Dina

- Myra Green, the submissive, regretful, and heartbroken mother of Joey Green

- Kelsey, a Chicagoan turned San Franciscan, an opera enthusiast, and Jason's former flame

- Phelan "Flynn" Butler, Joey Green's old pal and a fellow patient at the Oak Hill Mental Institution for the Criminally Insane

Neatly presented and garnished with a sprinkling of extras, the cast on these pages render superior performances and do their creative mother, Sloane, fantabulous justice.

BRAVO! BRAVO!

A twist here, a turn there, and outstanding in every definition of the word, the literature of Bianca Sloane—including the explosive narrative currently under review—never ceases to amaze and knock out my reader. And I stand by my declaration concerning her authorship: that she should be among the queens in the ever-evolving fictional genre of suspense. With this effort, Sloane has once again proven her greatness above and beyond the expected. And I applaud her immensely.

Dear reader, I would only advise you to read the two-part series, including *Every Breath You Take* and *Missing You*, in chronological order: for only then will you be sewn into the patchwork of its ingenuine storyline. For the same is as hauntingly beautiful as the city of Chicago at twilight.

Five hideously virulent stars.

Cat Ellington's review of Every Breath You Take Collection: Every Breath You Take & Missing You by Bianca Sloane

My rating: 5 out of 5 stars

Date read: December, 2015

GETTING STRAIGHT TO THE POINT.

As an ardent enthusiast of fictional works laden with drama and suspense, I'll admit that I am not one who is easily-roused; however, the fictional literature of Bianca Sloane—in its current entirety—has consecutively awed me.

To date, each one of Sloane's literary oeuvres has ascended above the expected standard of conventional fiction writing, hence proving that she is a gifted novelist of considerable ability. For hers is an incredible literary vision that is often-overlooked and shamefully underrated.

Every Breath You Take and *Missing You*, two magnificent narratives provided with their analyses within this volume, are a powerful five-star duo materially commanding praise and lofty recommendation.
And kudos to its authorship for blessing her newfound readers, including yours truly, with this additional double whammy of collected greatness.

Five neatly-packaged stars.

Chapter 6
Still Thriving

Cat Ellington's review of Gone by T.J. Brearton

My rating: 2 out of 5 stars

Date read: June, 2016

HAVE YOU SEEN THIS FAMILY?

An all-American family disappears without a trace. There are no letters left behind, and no one contacted family members. No nothing. It is as if they vanished into thin air. The authorities thus far have no leads and no motive. And there are only a few indications of their most recent activities in the abandoned home: an empty coffee mug sitting ever so casually on the deck, a teddy bear left alone on the floor of a child's bedroom, an unmade bed in the master bedroom, a bowlful of popcorn on the coffee table, and the garage door left wide open, among other things.

The standard family of four, including a father, a mother, and two children consisting of a son and a daughter, haven't been missing for very long, but they are missing. And any number of people, including their neighbors and their loved ones, would like to know what happened to them.

NEVER FEAR, DETECTIVE RONDEAU IS HERE!

Just existing since the death of his dearly beloved wife, Janice, Detective Jay Rondeau runs on two types of fuel: his job on the New Brighton police force and strong, black coffee.
Speaking of which, Rondeau is trying to figure out how he might remove a freshly-spilled coffee stain from his brand new pants when his subordinate and rookie cop, Eric Stokes, walks into his office with the day's special: a downed drone that was deliberately shot out of the sky by a paranoid schizophrenic and conspiracy theorist named Millard, whom, by the way, just so happens to be Rondeau's brother-in-law.
The disabled vessel now rests on the head detective's front lawn, and he must be on his way so that he may calm the twitchy and frazzled nerves of Millard.

Now, back to the missing family. The missing family? Well, as it turns out, they just so happen to be the semi-famous Kemp clan consisting of the writer, producer, and documentary filmmaker, Hutchinson Kemp, his wife Lily, and their two small children, toddler Maggie and baby William.
Because of their notability, news about the Kemp family is beginning to spread - like wildfire - in the media. And before hearing about the missing family via officer Stokes, Rondeau had never even heard of Hutchinson Hutch Kemp, much less about the industry in which he worked, which is typical because Jay Rondeau is just grizzled, average, and oblivious.

Stokes has given him the rundown on the Kemp situation. And Rondeau's number one priority now is to locate the missing filmmaker and his immediate family. But for our leading man—pun intended—it's not going to be that simple. Because the high-profile assignment will prove to be far more dangerous than Rondeau could have ever imagined.

THE MAN WHO KNEW TOO MUCH.

Unfortunately, Hutchinson Kemp, while filming one of his best environmental documentaries yet, had stumbled upon secrets that some individuals in the United States government would rather the public at large not know. And eager to produce an award-winning exposé, Hutchinson Kemp unknowingly endangered the lives of every member of his entire household, even from the head down to the least. And this is where Rondeau comes in. Here is where Detective Rondeau gets to play the hero.

And it would have perhaps been a good breakout performance for him were it not for such a lackluster script and an equally lackluster supporting cast.

SPEAKING OF WHICH.

The following co-star with Detective Rondeau on the uninteresting pages of this slow and tedious script:

- Dr. Connie Leifson, a head professor of sociology at New Brighton college and Millard's psychotherapist

- Addison Kemp, Hutchinson Kemp's sister, and his only sibling

- Peter King, a top deputy of the New Brighton Patrol Division

- Althea Bruin, a top deputy of the New Brighton Patrol Division and partner to Deputy Peter King—with whom the African-American Bruin is also involved in an interracial relationship

- Britney Silas, the CSI agent representing the forensics team

I'M SO GLAD IT'S OVER.

Hardly *'A Suspense Thriller With An Almighty Twist In The Tale'* is the novel currently under review.
On the contrary, my experience with *Gone* had been nothing short of exhaustive. And I couldn't conclude it quickly enough.

Perhaps to its author, T.J. Brearton—and maybe a handful of readers—*Gone* lives up to the proposition of its tagline. But the dialogue only served to drain my energy level.
On the other hand, as I sometimes like to say of some novels: It's not the best effort, but it has its moments. That sentiment should be applied here.

Happy reading, all.

Cat Ellington's review of See How They Run by Tom Bale

My rating: 3 out of 5 stars

Date read: June, 2016

THE TROUBLE WITH HARRY.

Award-winning filmmaker Harry French is just a quiet guy. Harry lives with his wife, Alice, and their baby daughter, Evie, in an English town called Brighton. Nothing out of the ordinary ever occurs in their quaint parts aside from the occasional alley cat squealing in the dead of night or the urban foxes that sometimes inspect the alleyway beneath the family's bedroom window in search of discarded dinner scraps. Their neighbors, a peaceful bunch who pretty much keep to themselves, go about their daily routines: work, shopping whenever necessary, holidays now and again, etc. Overall, Brighton is a pleasing community. And Harry and his small family enjoy dwelling there.

But as the curtains open, introducing the plot of this relatively entertaining—and somewhat suspenseful—conspiracy thriller, the quiet and simple life of Harry French is about to undergo a dreadfully sinister transformation due to no fault of his own. Harry French has not done what is evil, but the three gun-wielding masked men who have invaded his home in the middle of the night and stand idling at the foot of his bed while his wife and baby daughter lay sleeping soundly beside him, are not to be convinced otherwise.

A strange voice speaks and says, 'Wake up, sleepyhead.' For even in the darkened bedroom, he somehow *knows* that Harry is already awake. And soon, so is a terrified Alice.

The leader of the trio now speaks, asking the perplexed couple, 'Where is he? Renshaw. Edward Renshaw.'

While Harry and Alice have absolutely no knowledge of the person about whom the masked man queries, the home invader continues to press on, saying, 'You had a parcel. The parcel was addressed to Mr. E Grainger. It came to this address. 34 Lavinia Street.'

A frightened Harry and Alice try to explain to these men that there has been some confusion. They live on Lavinia Street, yes, but there is also Lavinia *Drive* and Lavinia Crescent. And that perhaps these men had the wrong address. Unfortunately, though, the couple is not as persuasive as they would like to believe. And this leads the three concealed gunmen to aim their weapons at the most precious asset of Harry and Alice French: the eighteen-month-old Evie.

With that, the French family's worst nightmare begins.

WHY, YOU SNEAKY BASTARD!

So who, exactly, is Edward Renshaw?

Edward Renshaw is the man who nearly got the innocent French family killed over something about which they know absolutely nothing.

Edward Renshaw is a man on the run from a pitiless group of armed murderers. He has something that they want, something they are willing to kill in cold blood to procure. But just what could that *something* be? Whatever it is, it

was enough for Edward Renshaw to take it and run for his worthless life. It was enough for him to address the parcel to a false residence—the French's—and then lie in wait to see what happened if and when the hired killers came looking for him. And they did.
They came in search of him. And he saw them.

A crook by trade, Edward Renshaw knowingly addressed the coveted package to the erroneous occupancy at 34 Lavinia Street. And while his would-be killers terrified the law-abiding French family, he sat biding his time and peering from the windows of another flat right across the road—at 34 Lavinia *Drive*.
But there is a special day for every individual dog in the land.

MISS MONROE – INTERNATIONAL WOMAN OF MYSTERY.

Out of nowhere, she appeared, wearing a wig to disguise her specification. She already knows about the home invasion that terrified Harry and Alice French only a few nights before. She even knows the identities of the ruthless home invaders. But who is she? And who's side is she truly on?
Enter Ruth Monroe, a woman who knows something—and something more than she's letting on. Harry French must now risk not only his own life but also that of his family. He now has to team up with the "questionable" Ruth Monroe to find out just how deep this puzzling well goes.

Who were the men that invaded his home looking for the man named Edward Renshaw? The man who threatened to cut his newborn baby's throat? Who is he? What is it that Renshaw has that they so desperately want? And just how much does this perplexing woman, Ruth, know about these men?

MEANWHILE…

Alice is on the prowl searching for the slick-as-oil stranger who nearly got her baby killed. And to start, she pays a kindly visit to her bored friend, Clare, who just so happens to live right next door to the flat into which the murderous madmen should have been breaking the night before. Clare claims that no one lives there, but how sure is she? Perhaps there could be someone living there unbeknownst to her: maybe Renshaw? Or is it *Grainger*? Or is it *Miller*? Whoever he is, and whatever his real name may be, there are a group of heartless killers on his trail. And he will do whatever it takes to keep from being captured by them, even if it means causing the deaths of a completely innocent family who were only trying to live out their lives.

YOU CAN RUN … BUT YOU CAN'T HIDE FOREVER.

People tend to make mistakes. That is why erasers exist. And in the case of the mysterious package sent to Harry and Alice French, it was not sent by mistake. It was callously deliberate. And it was set in motion by one Edward Renshaw, the man hiding in number 43.

Mr. Renshaw could only hope that his terrifying pursuers wouldn't be hip to the fact that Lavinia *Drive* ends at number 28 and that 34 Lavinia *Crescent* is only a business and not a living space.

Edward Renshaw bet the farm on their ignorance. He counted every dime on their confusion. And in his lowdown scheming, he caused the wrath of an entire criminal outfit to blow upon the heads of Harry, Alice, and Evie French.

Evie French, a newborn baby oblivious to the nightmare beginning to unfold in her loving parents' lives.
Evie French, the newborn baby who came this close to having her tender throat slit by a hired killer right before the eyes of her horrified parents.
Evie French, a beautiful eight-week-old baby girl who's clad in a pram suit and strapped in a baby carrier close to her mother's chest on the day that an infuriated Alice—with the mystery parcel in hand—finally confronts the evasive Edward Renshaw.

THE SUSPENSE BUILDS.

Unfortunate for the French family was the purposeful parcel delivery mixup. Even worse, however, is the harsh reality of the present situation. Alice finally knows who Edward Renshaw is. And the two of them, with baby Evie in tow, will now have to run as fast as they possibly can for the preservation of their contrary lives. Especially now that a deadly operative may have spotted Alice entering the block at number 43.

THE TERRIBLE NATHAN LAIRD.

No one knows of him, save his henchmen and those who utterly buckle at the mere mention of his name. And if one is even familiar with him in the first place, well, the chances are that the same individual is already on a wide-and-spacious path that leads on to obliteration. Reminiscent of "Tony Soprano," Nathan Laird has many enemies as he, himself, is an enemy to many. And counted among his many enemies is the woman named Ruth Monroe, the same woman with whom Harry French has just teamed up. Ruth Monroe is a woman of great anger. And Nathan Laird has stolen quite a bit more from her than just a happy home.

Revenge. Some say it's sweet.
But I say, only to the one who has been able to exact it.

THE WOMAN FROM GLOUCESTERSHIRE.

There is no better place to safely hide from the likes of Nathan Laird and his battalion of life-enders than the cozy little town of Cranstone in Gloucestershire. That is where Nerys Baxter, a woman somehow involved in it all, has chosen to settle down in her new life—far away from her former life of crookedness and corruption.
But rest does its best to steer clear of the wicked. And it's not long before the doorbell chimes—rang, of course, by an old associate from her not-too-distant past. It's Edward Renshaw. And not only Renshaw but also a woman—a strange woman—with a small baby in her possession.

The cunning past has returned to reacquaint itself with her. And Nerys is not in any position to shoo it away. Not unless she wants her whereabouts to become the knowledge of those from whom she has thus far been successful in concealing herself.
For she, too, has an awful lot to hide.

THE FUGITIVES.

They're all suddenly implicated now, Harry, Alice, Ruth, Edward, Nerys, and poor little Evie.
Aside from Edward, Nerys, and maybe even Ruth, no one knows what's inside of that ill-fated parcel. But whatever the contents, there is a dangerous man who wishes to retrieve it, regardless of Edward Renshaw's refusal to relinquish it: for the contents therein will serve to either save Mr. Renshaw's tawdry life or lead the way to its end. With that, he must stay on the run. And he must take hostages, hence Alice and baby Evie.

BE ANXIOUS FOR SOMETHING.

In the meantime, Harry French is missing both his wife and their baby girl. Unable to reach Alice on her cell, Harry is understandably a nervous wreck. But at least he's not alone; Ruth Monroe is there to keep him company. She's also there to entangle him in a deviously constructed web of deceit and double-dealing espionage. And where Harry French had not known much before, he knows too much now. They wouldn't dare allow him to walk away with an old, 'Oh, no harm, no foul, Harry.' No, of course not. For the bloodthirsty are just as parched for innocent blood as they are for that of the guilty.
And knowing this much, both Harry and Ruth must also flee for their lives—together.

On these subtle pages of English mystery and mayhem, Friday night arrives without a suitcase, and Sunday morning creeps in like a nun.

Man and wife and child become the night's prey—

See how they run.

THE PLAYERS.

Joining the passably talented ensemble of French, Renshaw, Baxter, Laird, and Monroe in this cozy but cold-hearted read are none other than the following:

- Niall Foster, a man who operates without either emotion or warning

- Darrell Bridge, a twin spirit of Niall Foster and a trusty henchman to the same

- Steve, Alice's adored uncle, and an all-around handyman

- Sam, another character on a first-name basis, a BAFTA Award-winning filmmaker, and Harry's business partner at LiveFire

- Michael Baxter, the loyal son of Nerys and a secretive man who is not at all what he seems

- Keri, a woman so obscure to the general public that she requires no last name; nevertheless, she is also heavily involved in the criminal drama

- Robyn Baxter, a passive wife to the mama's boy, Michael, and an unwitting daughter-in-law to Nerys

- Mark Vickery, yet another dangerous man on the hunt for Renshaw accompanied by a handsome reward

- Clare McIntosh, a good neighbor to the French's and a close friend of Alice

- Detective Inspector Dean Warley, the man who is supposedly investigating the French family home invasion. But is he?

- DC Sian Cassell, a partner to Detective Inspector Dean Warley and the woman who is supposedly assisting him with the investigation into the French family home invasion. But is she?

THE ANALYTICAL RUNDOWN.

Tom Bale presents a relatively enjoyable narrative with *See How They Run* as the effort, while not five-star superb, did manage to command my reader's interest until the very end.

Nicely paired with a glass of chilled white wine on a warm summer's day, *See How They Run* would be a perfect mystery thriller for fans of Louise Jensen and Robert Bryndza. And although I didn't find the plot to be all that explosive, even still, the script has its gripping moments and therefore should be considered generously recommended.
Happy reading, all.

Cat Ellington's review of Fatally Bound (McRyan Mystery Series, #4) by Roger Stelljes

My rating: 5 out of 5 stars

Date read: June, 2016

Being a woman whose residential ties extend to the Twin Cities, I immediately took an interest in the anecdote currently under review.

Fatally Bound was my thrilling introduction to the fiction of St. Paul native Roger Stelljes, respectively. And I can say, in a spirit of truth, that his style of writing is an "acquired taste." Indeed, the reader will be left with a sensational desire to consume more of Stelljes's work soon after concluding this dexterously-scribbled tale of furious bloodshed.

Dear reader? Shall we?

PAYBACK CAN BE DEADLY.

As this tale of enraged retribution gears up to emerge from its stalls with a blazing force, the reader is made privy to a woman's tearful and fatigued confession.

She is seated—bound to her chair with duct tape—before a large man who would be her killer. The man? At present, he is her menacing interrogator. He is a dark, looming force with whom it would not be in the woman's best interest to trifle.

He wants to know if she has told him everything. She insists that she has. But he is still not convinced. Again, the woman insists that she has told him *everything* about *everyone* included in his guttural queries. But her fearful (and tearful) confession is not wholly unconditional. It's for survival. *Her* survival, mind you.

As far as her interrogator is concerned, she's guilty. She always has been guilty, and she always will be. And not only her, but also her three buddies, her former college besties. They're all guilty as sin itself. And they must pay - these four women. They must pay - starting with her. Once again, he probes her, asking whether she has told him *everything*. And once again, she insists that she has.

His sharp and angry knife is the last thing she sees. And her voice begging him to spare her life is the last thing she hears.
Her happy-go-lucky life is soon no longer.

IT TAKES TWO.

Two long years have passed since he rid the Earth of two of them. Now only two remain. And he needs to relieve them both of their privileged lives on Earth as well. Yes, he will send them off, that they will once again be joined together with their cohorts in everlasting death.

They must pay; they all must pay.

HANNAH.

Hannah Donahue, an elementary school teacher and the daughter of a big-time political contributor, has settled down into a comfortable life in Dover, Delaware. And all is good. She loves her job, she loves her ridiculously expensive Audi A6, and she loves her cutesy little two-story home situated on its well-kempt street.
But *he* hates her. And *he* has been watching her every move until now.
Oh, how patient he has been, patient in his waiting. And now, the moment has come. The time has come for Hannah to pay the piper. And she must pay. She must pay for what she has done.
She must experience his wrath.
She, too, must die.

She, too, must die at the hands of his *Reaper*.

WE'RE DEALING WITH A SERIAL.

It doesn't take FBI Senior Supervisory Agent Aubrey Gesch and his partner, FBI Supervisory Agent Grace Delmonico, long to conclude that they have a serial killer on their hands. As they examine the familiar crime scenes, their conclusion becomes quite evident: each female victim was found bound with duct tape and staged in a fetal position with her abdomen sliced open in the shape of the Holy Cross.
Same perp? Absolutely. His or her identity? They haven't a clue. They do, however, have a moniker for the mystery perp - the result of a macabre signature left at each crime scene of wretched horror:

"Even as I have seen, they that plow iniquity, and sow wickedness, reap the same."
—The Reaper

HER LIFE MATTERS.

Although other women suffered brutally at the fierce hands of a suspected serial killer, it is not until Hannah Donahue—the daughter of the famous campaign contributor, William Donahue—loses her life in the same manner that members of the press come running. Almost immediately, their heinous howls reach the ears of James Thomson, er, *President* James Thomson. And before long, the Holy Cross murders—all of them, *but especially Hannah Donahue's*—become front-page and headline news nationwide.

William Donahue—the Stephen Cloobeck of this plot—is none too pleased with the FBI's current investigation. And he's threatening to make heads roll in Washington unless someone jumps through his fiery hoops at breakneck speed to bring the killer of his daughter, his *precious* daughter, to justice.

Unfortunately for President James Thomson, Bill Donahue's fierce tirade is towards him in particular. And now he must act – and fast.

THE LIVE WIRE.

Dara Wire is one busy bee, what with running her private security consulting firm and putting the finishing touches on her first co-authored book. A woman with heavy political ties to Washington because of the security handled by her firm during the Presidential elections, Dara Wire has become the most sought out security consultant in Washington. Indeed, the woman is in great demand with high-ranking officials and judges alike: whenever they call, Dara Wire answers. And her nonsense radar is forever on the up. That's why she's the woman for the tedious job at hand.

Incidentally, the co-author of the book Dara Wire is writing just so happens to be our leading man, Michael McKenzie "Mac" McRyan—the pride and joy of St. Paul Irish. He's also the perfect candidate—no pun intended—to assist her with the tedious job at hand.

THE BIG MAC.

Michael McKenzie McRyan is a beloved and highly respected legend in the St. Paul Police Department. Known as "Mac" to his equally valued peers in law enforcement, McRyan is a man who, outside of his work on the force, has done well for himself in the wake of selling his stake in a highly lucrative coffee shop. He's also working on a new book with his good friend, Dara Wire, and renovating an old Georgetown brownstone that he and his girlfriend, the former federal prosecutor Sally Kennedy, have just purchased in Washington, DC. The Georgetown digs will help Sally stay closer to the political action in her new job as White House Deputy Communications Director in the Thomson administration.

Mac is currently back on cop duty in Minnesota—investigating a series of home invasions targeting the ultra-rich—when he gets the call. It's Dara

with news about the suspected serial. She informs him that his legendary detective work will be most welcome in Washington as the influential Judge Dixon and FBI Director Mitchell themselves have personally summoned him. And if these two men, of all men, have personally requested his law enforcement services, Mac trusts that the situation must be dire.
Indeed, it is.

FOR THEY ALL HAVE SINNED.

It's anyone's guess who the so-called *Reaper* is. And with a ton of speculation blowing like airborne blood in the wind, the media feeding frenzy is now underway. And Michael McKenzie McRyan is now in town.
Meanwhile, a cold-hearted murderer sits watching it all, what all of the news coverage surrounding his inhumane crimes. And he can't help but relish it.

It was Hannah. His obliteration of her is what set off this nationwide manhunt. They're all searching for him now. But will they find him in time? The hotshot cop guy, who's he? Whoever the copper is, he's so certain that he'll catch him. He's so smug, this cop. They all are. But they had better act fast because he still has yet one final kill. And hers will be the most sensational murder of them all. One final sinner tramp. She must join the others; for they all have sinned.
He still has yet one final kill. One final sinner tramp. And if the hotshot cop and that security consultant chick think for one minute that they can stop him, well, he'll just have to obliterate them, too.

In all of their respective years in both law enforcement and security consulting, Mac McRyan and Dara Wire will soon realize that neither of them has ever seen such a murderer as the one who is called *"The Reaper."*

THE ANALYTICAL DENOUEMENT.

From Washington to Delaware to Pennsylvania to Maryland and back, Mac McRyan and Dara Wire are on the hunt for a cunning and unsparing serial killer who, thus far, has managed to remain two steps ahead of them.

Joining our starring leads in their investigative efforts is a considerable—and effective—cast of supporting players who help supply the energy to their power source by bringing the plot alive with raw intensity and a healthy dose of electric blue vibrancy:

- Charlie Flanagan, the hard-nosed St. Paul police chief who acts as a dearly loved father figure to Mac

- Martin Gonzalez, a Florida-based attorney - and the tall, wealthy love interest of Dara Wire

- Detective Dane Wente of the Dover PD, the lead investigator assigned to assist McRyan and Wire with the Hannah Donahue murder

- Lana Meister and Nicole Moore, fellow elementary school teachers and close friends of Hannah Donahue

- Wendy Jonas, an executive at Asia Pacific Banking Worldwide and a close friend of Hannah Donahue

- Cedric Lewis, a big-and-beefy MMA fighter, a cowardly batterer of women, and a bit player the reader will love to hate

- Wallace Llewellyn, a high-powered attorney - and a legendary Washington fixer

- Angelo Dorsett, the Harrisburg, Pennsylvania task force detective assigned to assist McRyan and Wire in their quest to catch a savage killer

- Sandy Faye, a pretty, petite, and popular news anchor—and a woman hunted

Complemented by the flawless performances of a small batch of bit players, including Brenda Bell, Alice Walton, Percy Whitlock, Pat Dye, Richard Lich, Paddy McRyan, Pat Riley, and Bobby Rockford, the top-billed cast of *Fatally Bound* is excellent. Mac McRyan and company will not only grip the reader's undivided attention from beginning to end but also lead the way to an enduring admiration for their creator, Roger Stelljes.

Mac McRyan is brilliant as our leading man. And Dara Wire will remind some readers of "Olivia Benson" in her role as our supporting lead.

Great job, Mr. Stelljes!

MY RECOMMENDATION.

Fatally Bound is a psychological thriller that will leave an imprint on the psyche of each reader. With this singular dialogue, we have ourselves an efficiently composed plot of fast-paced thrills, white-knuckled drama, and stomach-churning suspense. And for what it's worth, I wholeheartedly enjoyed every kibble and bit of it.
Those of you who foster a passion for psychological thrillers centered around the murderous mayhem of serial killers are sure to love *Fatally Bound*. And while the subject matter is not uncommon in its class, even still, the narrative offers yet another entertaining take on the theme. Consider it highly commendable of my most generous recommendation.

Five knick-knack-paddywhack stars.

Cat Ellington's review of Squall by Sean Costello

My rating: 5 out of 5 stars

Date read: July, 2016

BABY, IT'S COLD OUTSIDE.

If there were ever a staggering tale of crime fiction published in the beloved field of literature, it would be greater than safe to say that Sean Costello's masterwork, *Squall*, is such a one.

On these Canadian-based pages of criminality, death, destruction, and treacherous dealing, the love of many has grown ice cold. And in with a Northern squall, blows Satan himself—to be an evil trial unto the blameless.

DALE & RONNIE.

In a spirit of strife, the script introduces the reader to two of its top cast members, Dale Knight and Ronnie Saxon—who, by the way, portray lovers in this fictional life. At present, Dale and Ronnie are en route with a casual Dale at the wheel and a contentious Ronnie in the passenger seat scoffing at her man about his lowly position within his older brother's criminal organization.

Ronnie? Well, she wants more out of life. She's tired of having to live from hand to mouth in a dump, while big Ed Knight lives like the kingpin he is in the grandest of style and luxury. She's sick and tired of being sick and tired. She wants more. And her verbal frustration is rising like hot steam, scorching the ears of the passive errand boy, Dale. And Dale? Well, he keeps on repeating the same old tired lines to Ronnie: *Ed's just showing him the ropes. He'll promote Dale soon. Ed started as an errand boy himself, blah, blah, blah.*

But Ronnie—a hardened coke head who is as catty as they come—ain't buyin' it. She has herself a little plan, and that is to rip ol' big Ed off. All Dale has to do is take his brother's stash and flee to a warmer environment, say, Miami or someplace else exotic. Because right now, *any* place, particularly in the United States, would be better than his and her current predicament in the frigid provinces of their native Canada.

And while she makes her conniving thoughts known to Dale—verbally—there is only one (important) thing that Ronnie has foolishly forgotten. The stash that she so desperately wants to steal? It does not belong to Ed. It belongs to Randall Copeland. And Randall Copeland is not a man who suffers fools gladly.

Randall Copeland has long withstood many enemies in his specialty—which is that of the Canadian drug trade—and he has every intention of continuing in his tradition.

That is what the dirty birdie named Ronnie Saxon has failed—in her desperation—to remember.
But desperate people always find a way.

THE CALM BEFORE THE STORM.

It's cold outside, a wicked storm is on the horizon, and bush pilot Tom Stokes, the co-founder of *Stokes Aviation*, is gearing up to celebrate his thirty-first birthday.

Incidentally, Tom Stokes is also our leading man. And he's quite a guy.

While peace is still enjoying its time with us, Tom awakes to face the day in his cozy cabin on the lake - the same cozy cabin that he shares with his most precious valuables: his very pregnant wife, Mandy, and their five-year-old son, Steve—the latter who just so happens to share a birthday with his affectionate dad.

The Stokes clan does just fine, managing the lucrative real estate business built by Tom's father. They also own a fleet of lake cabins, cargo transport, and a year-round flight school.

Indeed, all things are sweet, loving, and comfortable on the Stokes' home front. And peace is at liberty to revel in its leisurely dominance.

Whence cometh the monkey wrench - tossed into its fray?

THE STORM CLOUDS START TO ROLL IN.

After a cold-hearted murder, Dale and Ronnie are now on the run. They've got some cash flow, and they've got a whole lot of dope. But even still, neither ill-gotten duo can help the lawless couple escape the incoming storm. The roads are as treacherous as the humans' hearts, and the only safe place for them to lay low—until Old Man Winter gets done settling his snowy score—is a vacant cabin on the lake owned by Ed and Dale's uncle, Frank, whom, by the way, is out of town for the season.

But while the wicked strut the Earth making plans, Father God is seated on His inimitable throne of supreme dominion in the Kingdom of Heaven - laughing.

Whatever is to go awry will. And guilt has sidled up to Dale to trouble his conflicted mind. He knows he should call Ed, but he does not. He knows he needs to call his brother and explain everything, but he does not. And the guilt is building: it nags and nags until it finally breaks him, and he eventually calls his dad, er, his big brother, Ed, to explain the situation from earlier in the day. In Dale's mind, he wants to make it right. But Dale should have held his peace. He should not have called Ed, but he did. And before long, Ed discovers the location of his younger sibling: uncle Frank's place.

AM I MY BROTHER'S KEEPER?

Self-preservation is the name of the game where the corrupt and murderous Ed Knight is concerned. If truth be told, he'd have his own mother's throat cut to save himself. And if one would be willing to put to death the very person from whose loins he or she spewed, what is to become of anyone else?
What Dale didn't understand is that two of the most lethal and terrifying goons known to the crooked and perverse, namely Sanj and Summit Sengupta, have already been given their orders—from the top down—to search and destroy. And those in the proverbial crosshairs? Dale Knight and Ronnie Saxton.

THE EYE OF THE STORM MAKES LANDFALL.

Had it been up to him, Tom Stokes would have stayed home with Mandy and had a proper breakfast, including the standard cup of piping hot, perfectly brewed java. But no, he had to fly a plane out to check on the damage sustained by one of their properties. The cabin is in disarray, sure. But Tom has a duty—as the property owner—to board up the smashed in windows to keep out the riff-raff wildlife. It'll be an easy task, what to board up the broken window, tidy up a bit, and head on back home. But Old Scratch? Well, he stands in the distance, watching the physical realm from his accursed place in the spiritual realm. And there's always a human being ripe for the picking.

On this particular day, he perceives three potential victims in Dale Knight, Ronnie Saxton, and Tom Stokes; and he breaks forth to cause a ferocious collision between them.

THE CRASH.

With his work done, Tom Stokes heads home to enjoy his joint birthday festivities with his little boy, Steve. Friends and family are eagerly awaiting his return, but Old Scratch—the party pooper that he is—blows in through a strong and blustery squall, forcing Tom's hand to make an emergency landing.

The crash landing is inevitable, taking into account the extreme weather conditions. But it's also unfortunate under the impending circumstances.

In the distance, Tom's engine roars, faltering. And none other than the ears of Ronnie Saxton can hear it. Indeed, while she's blowing her nose in one type of snow, Tom's cruising Cessna is headed downward to skid into the depths of snow of a different variety.

AN UNLIKELY PAIR.

Dale only wants to get high and forget his troubles. He's a dead man; he knows it: but Dale doesn't want to die. Dale wants to live a clean, healthy, and happy life. He dreams of opening a business, a pizzeria. That's all Dale Knight has ever wanted. And he's sitting in a tub of bathwater deep in thought about where his miserable life is going when the bathroom wall explodes, suddenly. A small aircraft crashes in, making an impact with the tub and trapping Dale underwater. He's going to drown. He knows it: this is the way he's going out. Or is it?

Here is where the two most unlikely of men come to meet for the very first time. Tom saves Dale's life, but not without a price.

Tom Stokes does not yet know that the life he has just saved is an amoral one. And rather than going home to enjoy his 31st birthday with his happy friends and family, Tom Stokes has now found himself unequally yoked with the scourge of the land. The same who are already on their way to Hell and don't necessarily mind taking the upstanding—and law-abiding—Tom down with them.

And for this reason, the life Tom must save now is his own.

ANOTHER STELLAR EFFORT.

With *Squall*, the patently shrewd Sean Costello has once again outdone himself!

A captivating tale, *Squall* quickly snatches the reader into its icy-cold grasp and refuses to let go until nothing remains of the viewer but speechless mesmerization and jaw-dropping awe.

Co-starring Captain Dan Tremblay of the Air and Marine Search and Rescue Unit, Redneck Ricky, and an amber-eyed mountain cougar with a taste for human blood, *Squall* is an effort with which I found it tremendously difficult to part ways. And I guess that many other readers will share this sentiment.

THE ANALYTICAL VERDICT.

Blessed with dexterous penmanship, award-worthy performances, a perfect pace, and plenty of ruthless suspense, *Squall* comes highly commended and even more so recommended—especially for the literary thrill-seeker.

Five gusty-and-blustery stars.

Cat Ellington's review of Sandman by Sean Costello

My rating: 5 out of 5 stars

Date read: July, 2016

THE KILLING OF JULIE BRITT.

Seventeen-year-old Julie Britt is terrified. And she should be, considering that she suffers from malignant hyperthermia, which is a debilitating condition that causes her body's temperature to rise higher than the standard for a healthy human being.

Unfortunately, Julie lost her older sister to this condition years ago, and she's no stranger to its life-threatening effects. But because she is experiencing some chronic pain associated with her condition—in addition to a ruptured appendix—Julie has been advised to undergo a specific surgical procedure that will provide her with some much-needed relief. However, there is only one problem: the anesthesia. Julie Britt is afraid of being anesthetized. She wants more than anything not to lose consciousness because that's what happened with her sister, only seven years of age at the time of *her* death. Julie tells the understanding nurse who is transporting her stretcher to the operating room that she's okay, it's only a cramp, and she doesn't need surgery. But the nurse is not convinced. She assures Julie Britt that everything will be just fine, Julie's anesthetist knows about her condition, and there's no need to worry. Comforting words, yes, but not enough to ease the dreadful panic ripping at the psyche of a very nervous Julie Britt. Her transport—by way of a stretcher—to operating room 5 mocks and scoffs at her fear. And not even the soothing words of her anesthetist, Dr. Rob Hardie, can fend off her terrors. Julie Britt is nearly in tears as she continues to plead, but Dr. Hardie assures her that everything will be fine. Her appendix is ruptured, and the medical team needs to remove it. There is no other way. Julie Britt knows this. She doesn't like it, but she is without any other choice.

Dr. Rob Hardie readies his anxious patient for the anesthetic, and Julie calms a bit. The spinal anesthetic will only *freeze* Julie, not put her to sleep. And once Dr. Hardie inserts the needle into her lower back, it only takes moments for the anesthesia to go into effect. Julie can feel the warm rush, the pain now escaping her. She even makes a request: Music.

There, there, it's okay, the relaxing medicine seems to say. *Just relax, Julie.* It practically coddles. *Relax.*

Before long, Julie Britt slips off into the inevitable state of unconsciousness. Everything is fine. Her monitors are in place, and her blood pressure is good. Her heart rate is on point, and so are her respirations. Indeed, she's in good hands with Dr. Hardie, who is alerted to her core temperature at all times. Satisfied that his patient is finally at ease and resting peacefully, Dr. Hardie must leave her to answer nature's call. And he instructs his nurse, Ellie, to summon another anesthesiologist to hold down the fort while he's away. But rather than watching over the awaiting patient, the substitute tampers with Julie's IV, shutting it off and injecting a synthetic compound into the bag of IV solution. Unfortunately, no one in the operating room witnesses his evil action. And Dr. Hardie soon returns to the OR to begin his procedure.

From there, all horrifying hell breaks loose in the operating room.
While she may appear to be sedated and insentient, Julie Britt is not.
Now gasping and convulsing, Julie Britt, despite her plunging pulse, is slowly regaining consciousness and becoming fully aware of what's happening around her. And although she's helpless to do or say anything about it—due to her inability to move and speak—Julie Britt can see, hear, and *feel*.
The medical equipment is now malfunctioning. And Dr. Hardie is barking orders at his team. He's desperately trying to administer oxygen, but she's suffocating. Julie's chest is tight, and she feels so hot. *So hot*. She's suffocating. She's also paralyzed, and her limbs are stiff. She's now flatlining, and Dr. Hardie is panicking. Julie can see the panic in his eyes. *It's all in his eyes*. He's desperately trying to save her. And by any means necessary, he will. Then he orders a tracheostomy.

A tracheostomy? Oh, dear God, they are going to cut her throat. She knows it. She has to get away, but she can't move. She can't move a muscle.

The attending surgeons call a code blue as the chaos erupts all around her. She's alive and paralytic, but the monitors indicate otherwise. Dr. Hardie has just asked for the scalpel.

The scalpel.

With that, Julie Britt can only plead for help. But no one can hear her petrified cries for help. They're only in her mind. Inevitably, the razor-sharp blade slices into her tender flesh, and every nerve in her body explodes in response. Her throat now filled with blood, Julie Britt is experiencing the worst kind of horror. She can feel death's covetousness as it makes haste to break in and steal her life away. And throughout her terrifying and unimaginably painful ordeal, only two people in the world know that she's sentient: Julie herself and her killer.

While Julie Britt's eternal soul is parting ways with her butchered and ravaged body, her killer stands watching from the Plexiglas panels of a darkened observation booth right above operating room 5.

Unflinching. Unblinking. Unemotional.
An effortless (and ruthless) kill - with more to come.

Unflinching. Unblinking. Unemotional.

ENTER SANDMAN.

As this soot-hearted tale of menacing suspense, engrossing thrills, and cunning mystery comes out from behind a blood-stained cubicle curtain to reveal itself to the reader, we become acquainted with a formidable ensemble led by our leading lady, Jenny Fallon. A woman with so much love to give, Jenny is the privileged wife of Dr. Jack Fallon - and the adoptive mother of fourteen-year-old Kim Fallon.

The family of three live well, but there is a healthy level of dysfunctionality between them, where Jack and Kim are concerned.

If it were not already enough that Kim is not their natural daughter, Jack is also annoyed with her excess body weight and her braces. She will never be good enough for him. Both she and Jenny know this. But that doesn't stop her from trying to win his affections. Jenny, on the other hand, loves Kimberly Anne with every fiber of her being. And she has never ceased telling the child as much.

The two are quite a team, Jenny and Kim Fallon. And while Jack spends much of his time at the hospital, where he serves as the head of the anesthesia department, Jenny—who is four months pregnant, by the way—and Kim make the most of their mother/daughter time at their palatial, albeit atmospherically tense, home.

This day is not unlike any other as Jenny and Kim dance around the house to happy music, laugh, hug and enjoy themselves. It's just another fun-filled day shared until the phone rings. Jack has called to give Jenny the sobering news about the horrible incident involving Julie Britt's death in the OR at the Med Center.

The news is miserable. And the girl's parents are devastated as they should very well be. But no member of the faculty is more overwhelmed with grief than Dr. Rob Hardie – who will most definitely have to face the disciplinary board in the wake of the tragedy.

Quite naturally, the scene at the hospital is chaotic and rampant. But it's not going to stop the Fallon's from carrying on with a planned weekend get-together at their posh lakeside cottage.

Faulty medical equipment and death resulting from it aside, the show must go on. And with Kim having a sleepover at the home of the Goodmans, it most certainly will.

RICH PEOPLE PROBLEMS.

Al Sutton is the guest of honor at Fallon's weekend retreat. Jack Fallon is grooming the thirty-two-year-old medical professional, of great distinction, for a top position within his highly-ranked department at the Med Center. Also invited to the cottage for a couple of days of rest-and-relaxation are Dr. Will Armstrong (the deputy chief of the anesthesia department at the Med Center) and his beautiful wife, Nina, and Dr. Paul Daw (a psychiatrist with a penchant for young, voluptuous women) and his date, Cerise.

The wealthy adults try to enjoy themselves, but the devil is not content to allow it. One can count on Will Armstrong to ruin an enjoyable evening, what with his notorious insecurities and jealousy.
Yes, his petite wife, Nina, is indeed a lovely woman. But God forbid another man even smiles at her.
Al Sutton is not only smart but funny. And Nina makes the awful mistake of laughing just a little too hard at his jokes. That's all it takes for Will to break up their little shindig and demand Nina to get her things so that they can leave and go home.
Meanwhile, Paul Daw and Cerise strive to make love that won't oblige due to Paul's erectile dysfunction. And Jack Fallon, a megalomaniac was there ever one born, is interested in doing anything but tending to his attentive—and emotionally battered—wife, Jenny.

Yes, they all have money—and plenty of it, I might add—but their worldly lives are problematic.

Jenny is a high-risk pregnancy: she has already suffered three miscarriages. Jenny does her best to hold it all together, although she knows that one wrong word can tear it all apart. She loves the comforts that her marriage to a prominent doctor provides, but she hates the eggshells that she has to walk on to keep the peace.
She only wants them to be a happy family. That's all.
Is that too much to ask?

A KILLER AMONG US.

Concerning our male leads, if one thing is not irritating them, something else is. And that would include the wreaking of cold-blooded havoc in their professional setting.

Sufficient for the moment is a savage killer in their midst.

Someone on staff at their fine institution is murdering patient after patient after patient - in the most heinous of ways. And while it is up to our doctors to find out who that antagonistic someone is, the task won't be easy. But then again, it never is when the killer is right under your nose. When he or she is the very one you would least expect.

A COMPLEX REIGN OF TERROR.

Indeed, Sean Costello's Canadian-based *Sandman* is one of the best anecdotes ever composed in its respective genre. Having read dozens of extremely-intense and heart-pounding tales scribbled by some of the best-loved authors of the set, it's safe to say that *Sandman* will go down in literary history as being one of the most blood-fermenting of them all.

A DELECTABLE BLEND OF SCRIPT AND CAST.

Blessed with superior range, the hard-hearted *Sandman* at once commands the reader's interest and holds it captive over an unstoppable storyline. Indeed, the fiction defies a reader's rest by tempting the same to remain abreast of both its outstanding storyline and the flawless performances rendered by a dynamic cast of supporting players, including:

- Dr. Ellen Kolb, the eccentric coroner

- Tracy Goodman, a slimmer, cuter, and more popular irritant to the chubby, average, and unpopular Kim Fallon

- Ben Crabtree, another lost soul for whom it would have been better, had he perished in the womb than to have ever been born at all

- Sam Goodman, a self-loathing supreme court judge and a dismissive father to the rebellious Tracy Goodman

- Dr. Craig Walsh, an obstetrician to Jenny Fallon and a gentle comforter

- Richard Dickerson/R. J. Kale, a world-famous artist, a long-lost love, and an angel in disguise

- Harry Katz, the ear, nose, and throat doctor by whom Will Armstrong is irked

- Mark Blumstein, a no-nonsense attorney at law and close associate of Nina Armstrong

- Wes Fransen, the lead detective investigating a series of suspicious murders at the Med Center

Rounding out this fabulous cast of characters are a small group of equally adept—and just as memorable—bit players: Emily Quinn, Niles McRae, Jerry Tilton, Ryan Hirsh, Theodore Harris, Claudia Rider Charlie Haid, Robin Jeep Elfman, Peter Chartrand, Peach the Cat, and five-year-old twin brothers, Jeffrey and Gerry Armstrong, who portray the children of Will and Nina Armstrong, respectively.

A REITERATION OF PRAISE.

Passionately recommended, *Sandman* is the sort of callous fiction that is sure to have its readers stewing in a broth of terror, revenge, anger, rage, hatred, misery, sadness, disgust, and nail-biting apprehension. The narrative is a masterpiece, even from its acidic beginning to its shattering end. And it should not be disregarded but approached with caution.

Five double-edged stars.

**THAT CONCLUDES *REVIEWS BY CAT ELLINGTON:
THE COMPLETE ANTHOLOGY, VOL. 3***

Until next time...

Coming September 2019

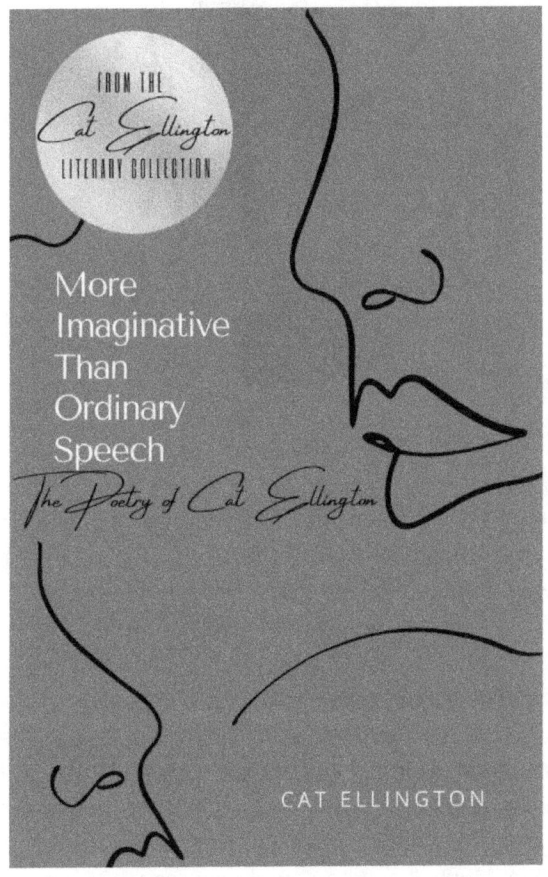

More Imaginative Than Ordinary Speech: The Poetry of Cat Ellington
Imprint: Quill Pen Ink Publishing
Cover Tint: Purple Pleasure

About the Author

Cat Ellington is an American songwriter, casting director, poet, author, and entrepreneur from Chicago, IL. She is best known for her creative contributions to the diverse industries and fields of music, movies, art, and literature.

Cat Ellington's professional credits list a collection of nonfiction books, including the Reviews by Cat Ellington series, The Making of Dual Mania, More Imaginative Than Ordinary Speech, Memoirs in Gogyohka, and You Can Quote Me On That. In film and music, Ellington's credentials include her work on the psychological thriller, "Dual Mania," and its soundtrack--on which she wrote five original songs: "The Book of Us," "I'm Still in Love," "Something in Your Eyes," "Gett Out," and "I Do."

Outside of her professional element, the award-winning creative enjoys reading, listening to music, cooking, collecting vintage and modern charm bracelets, watching movies and classic TV shows, sailing, jet-skiing, playing tennis, and eating frozen yogurt -- lots of it.

Cat Ellington on Amazon: Books, Biography, Blog, Audiobooks, Kindle

Cat Ellington at the Award-Winning Boutique Domain

Cat Ellington on Goodreads

Cat Ellington at the Review Period with Cat Ellington

Cat Ellington at IMDb

www.ingramcontent.com/pod-product-compliance
Lightning Source LLC
Chambersburg PA
CBHW031355040426
42444CB00005B/294